WHITE HORSES OVER FRANCE

Robin Hanbury-Tenison

White Horses
OVER FRANCE

From the Camargue to Cornwall

GRANADA
London Toronto Sydney New York

Granada Publishing Limited
8 Grafton Street, London W1X 3LA

Published by Granada Publishing 1985

British Library Cataloguing in Publication Data
Hanbury-Tenison, Robin
White horses over France:
from the Camargue to Cornwall.
1. France—Description and travel—1975–
I. Title
914.4′04838   DC29.3

ISBN 0-246-12529-2

Photoset by Rowland Phototypesetting Limited
Bury St Edmunds, Suffolk
Printed in Great Britain by
Mackays of Chatham Limited

The poem 'Horses on the Camargue' by Roy Campbell
is reproduced by permission of Fransisco Campbell Custodio
and Ad. Donker (Pty) Limited

FOR
Thibert and Tiki

And I saw Heaven opened, and behold a White Horse.

Revelations 19: 11

Good luck to You,
Good luck to Me,
Good luck to all the White Horses I see

Old Sussex saying

Should not this best garden of the world,
Our fertile France, put up her lovely visage?

Shakespeare, Henry VI, Part I

Now the great winds shoreward blow;
Now the salt tides seaward flow;
Now the wild white horses play,
Champ and chafe and toss in the spray.

Matthew Arnold, The Forsaken Merman

Contents

Acknowledgements ix
Map of the Journey x

1 Crin Blanc 1
2 The Camargue 12
3 En Route via Bulls 21
4 The Magic Begins to Work 33
5 *La Vie à Cheval* 42
6 *'Vos chevaux vous attendent, Monsieur'* 53
7 Caves, Birds and Balloons 61
8 Through Rural France 72
9 Touffou 83
10 Châteaux and Wine 90
11 Michael's Chapter 97
12 Louella's Chapter 102
13 The Nantes–Brest Canal 107
14 The Channel and Home 118

Appendix I: Départements Visited En Route 126
Appendix II: Chronology of the Journey 127
Appendix III: The Camargue Horse 129
Index 131

Horses on the Camargue BY ROY CAMPBELL

In the grey wastes of dread,
The haunt of shattered gulls where nothing moves
But in a shroud of silence like the dead,
I heard a sudden harmony of hooves,
And, turning, saw afar
A hundred snowy horses unconfined,
The silver runaways of Neptune's car
Racing, spray curled, like waves before the wind.
Sons of the Mistral, fleet
As him with whose strong gusts they love to flee,
Who shod the flying thunders on their feet
And plumed them with the snortings of the sea;
Theirs is no earthly breed
Who only haunt the verges of the earth
And only on the sea's salt herbage feed –
Surely the great white breakers gave them birth.
For when for years a slave,
A horse of the Camargue, in alien lands,
Should catch some far-off fragrance of the wave
Carried far inland from his native sands,
Many have told the tale
Of how in fury, foaming at the rein,
He hurls his rider; and with lifted tail,
With coal-red eyes and cataracting mane,
Heading his course for home,
Though sixty foreign leagues before him sweep,
Will never rest until he breathes the foam
And hears the native thunder of the deep.
But when the great gusts rise
And lash their anger on these arid coasts,
When the scared gulls career with mournful cries
And whirl across the waste like driven ghosts:
When hail and fire converge,
The only souls to which they strike no pain
Are the white-crested fillies of the surge
And the white horses of the windy plain.
Then in their strength and pride
The stallions of the wilderness rejoice;
They feel their Master's trident in their side,
And high and shrill they answer to his voice.
With white tails smoking free,
Long streaming manes, and arching necks, they show
Their kinship to their sisters of the sea –
And forward hurl their thunderbolts of snow.
Still out of hardship bred,
Spirits of power and beauty and delight
Have ever on such frugal pastures fed
And loved to course with tempests through the night.

Acknowledgements

To make a complete list of the many people who helped us so freely on our way across France would be impossible. Often we never knew their names but it was their kindness and hospitality which made it all possible. A few people must, however, receive special thanks. Jean-François Turquay and Henri Villedieu for finding us Thibert and Tiki; Messrs Abbott & Polden, Veterinary Surgeons of Bodmin, for putting together a much-used medical pack; Nigel Winser of the Royal Geographical Society for lending us a tent; Patrick Duncan of the Station Biologique de la Tour du Valat; Frank Fauvet of St Laurent d'Aigouze for exceptional generosity; above all, Maggie Skeaping, who not only inspired us to go in the first place, and introduced us to everyone in the Camargue, but gave invaluable advice throughout the planning stages and even lent me John's saddle.

ANTE

l'Association Nationale pour le Tourisme Equestre, La Randonnée et l'Equitation de Loisirs

> 15, Rue de Bruxelles – 75009 Paris
> Tel: 281.42.82

For information on riding in France, where horses may be hired and the addresses of equestrian experts throughout the country, ANTE should be contacted. They produce an invaluable booklet each year called Tourisme Equestre en France.

N

ENGLISH CHANNEL

Bodmin Moor
Maidenwell
Liskeard
Torpoint
PLYMOUTH
R Tamar
R Tavy

0 Km   150
0 M   100

● PARIS

St Pol-de-Leon
Roscoff
Morlaix
Carhaix-Plouguer
Taulé
Côtes-du-Nord
BREST
Finistère
Quimper
Morbihan
Pontivy
Josselin
Malestroit
RENNES
Lorient
Vannes
Quiberon
Carnac
Redon
Blain
ST NAZAIRE
NANTES
Loire-Atlantique

ST MALO
Le Mont-St Michel

LE MANS

Champtoceaux
Maine-et-Loire
ANGERS
Saumur
TOURS
Loire
Fontevraud-l'Abbé
Chinon
Richelieu
Indre-et-Loire
Vienne
Châtellerault
Touffou
Bonneuil-Matours
POITIERS
Chauvigny
L'Isle Jourdain
Vienne
Haute-Vienne
Charente
Confolens
LIMOGES
Rochechouart
Châlus
Jumilhac-le-Grand
Corrèze

CLERMONT-FERRAND

● LYON

Rhône

ATLANTIC
OCEAN

Dordogne
Dordogne
Souillac
Terrasson-la-Villedieu
Rocamadour
Gramat
Figeac
Villeneuve
Cajarc
Rodez
Salles-Curan
Nîmes
P de Salars
Millau
Gard
AVIGNON
Aveyron
le Caylar
Castries
Arles
Bouch du-Rhô
BORDEAUX
Tarn-et-Garonne
la Cavalerie
St Guilhem-le-Désert
Aniane
MONTPELLIER
Aigues-Mortes
le Grau-du-Roi
Camargue
Stes Maries-de-la-Mer
MARSEILLE
TOULOUSE
Aveyron

Golfe du Lion

MEDITERRANEA

White Horses over France

1

Crin Blanc

From the study window of my farm in Cornwall I can see the rolling
hills and craggy tors of Bodmin Moor. The sheep move across a steep
field cropping the grass, still crisp with morning frost. Beyond, on the
open moorland, the cattle move through the gorse and bracken in
search of rough grazing. Across the garden, beyond a short stretch of
post-and-rail fence – our two white horses. Their coats have grown thick
and shaggy making them both look like moorland ponies. But when I
call them from the window they hurry over to the fence, looking in my
direction with eager, hopeful expressions on their faces. It almost seems
that they want to be ridden, perhaps to set off again on another long
journey. More likely they are simply hoping that I will bring them a
carrot each and yet we understand each other so well now that I know
there is more to it than that.

They are Camargue horses, stocky and plain by normal equestrian
standards, but with exceptional intelligence and character. They are
probably the first horses of their breed ever to come to Britain and they
have proved to be exactly what we need on the farm. At rest they look
a mess and people wonder why we bothered to go so far to find them.
But as it says in the official description of the Camargue horse, 'He saves
his nervous energy for action – that is why when at rest he may appear
uncoordinated and sleepy.' Besides, they represent the fulfilment of a
dream and bringing them home was in itself an adventure.

I suppose it all began with seeing *Crin Blanc* years ago as a child. It is one
of those films which practically everyone in Europe seems to remember,
either through having seen it or through hearing about it. Mention the
Camargue, that wild, marshy region between the two mouths of the
Rhône and half-learnt geography lessons provide a picture of flamingos
flying over a landscape of reeds and water, sun and wind. Flocks of
ducks and waders migrate there as do rollers, bee-eaters and hoopoes;
dykes and canals intersect both dry and wetlands; men live in small
white thatched houses tending fierce black bulls and growing rice,
asparagus and grapes; and they ride on wild white horses.

Crin Blanc is the archetype epitomising the virtues and the mysteries of all Camargue horses; the stallion so wild that the tough *gardians* are unable to catch it. A lonely fisher boy who watches them fail is told by the horses' owner in a fit of pique after an unsuccessful chase that if he can catch Crin Blanc he can have him. When he has done so, horse and boy becoming devoted to each other in an alien world, perfidious man predictably renegues and the film ends with them swimming out to sea together chased by wicked *gardians* to vanish at last beneath the waves.

The film is a black and white classic and was made in 1953 by Albert Lamorisse, with Alain Emery starring as the boy. The same team later made *The Red Balloon*, this time naturally in colour, which became even better known.

As a child in Ireland I rode gigantic hunters across terrifying country where the hedges and ditches were huge and the fields, both human and arable, were tiny. I was sent to pony club camp where I learnt a bit about how to look after a horse and later I rode in lots of local point-to-points on a gallant but not very fast horse called Outcry. In those days there were often as many as twenty or thirty starters in a race over a course where the jumps were natural obstacles and only wide enough for two or three horses at a time. It was more like the Palio at Siena than a modern race. I even spent one school holidays as a stable lad with the great Irish trainer Dan Moore and later rode over some of the Irish Grand National course at Fairyhouse in the maiden race before the great event. The jumps were so big it felt like flying, with the same sickening lurch in the stomach on coming down for a bad landing. Outcry and I never won a race, but we were placed a few times and I learnt to ride.

As an agricultural student at Cirencester I bought a white Arab pony from a British regiment. They had acquired him on the racecourse at Baghdad and he had subsequently been adopted by the commanding officer's wife. She taught him dressage and show jumping as well as hunting him and playing polo on him. When my first wife Marika and I moved to Cornwall we managed to pack all our possessions into a small borrowed horsebox in which Najah, then aged seven, stood surrounded by chairs, tables, a swing seat and our bed. He turned into a wonderful cattle pony and never faltered for nearly twenty years until an exceptionally cold winter when he suddenly gave up.

I always dreamed of fetching more like him from Persia or elsewhere in the Middle East and for years it was 'the next expedition but one' in my travel plans. Whenever I spoke about it people's imaginations seemed fired by the idea and they begged to be allowed to come too. In many ways, I found, it was a more appealing concept than the most exotic exploration of tropical forests or islands. Although the moment was never right and the Middle East was always in too much turmoil, I always knew that one day I would do it.

Then, in the summer of 1983, I went with my son Rupert and my second wife Louella to stay with Quentin Crewe in Provence. Not very far away lay the Camargue, a part of France I had never visited but which conjured up familiar, half-remembered pictures, especially those of Crin Blanc and the other white horses. Perhaps they were the answer. I was certainly in need of two new horses on the farm as poor old Najah was long dead and the two we had were barely able to handle the daily round of checking the moors for strays and sick animals as well as the exhausting round-ups when we had to bring in the cattle for market, or clear the hill of sheep for dipping. They were also both getting on in years, being seventeen and eighteen years old.

We all went to tea with Maggie Skeaping, widow of the great British horse painter and sculptor John Skeaping. They had kept a herd of Camargue horses for years, becoming involved in the lives of several leading *gardian* families, and if anyone could give me sound advice it was Maggie. I put my crazy idea to her, fully expecting to be told of innumerable obstacles to prevent an Englishman buying Camargue horses and riding them home.

'Do it!' she said without a moment's hesitation. 'John and I always said we'd ride some of our beautiful horses back to England, but there was never time. As far as I know no one has taken a Camargue horse across the Channel but they should suit you perfectly; they are as tough as nails and of course wonderful with cattle. That's what they are bred for. And it's the best possible way to see France.'

She was right and I'm very grateful to her.

From then on there was no doubt in my mind that it would happen. It was simply a matter of making plans, something I have always greatly enjoyed. Once an expedition is conceived there are, as every traveller knows, three distinct phases to be gone through; planning, execution and aftermath, each perhaps more pleasurable than the last. In this case planning was extraordinarily easy, almost miraculous. Detailed enquiries with the relevant authorities in the UK produced the astonishing information that, unlike all other mammals, horses can be imported virtually without restrictions. Although they can get rabies and many do in Eastern France and across the border in Germany (but not yet in the Camargue), there is no quarantine for them. All that is required is a veterinary certificate stating that the horse is in good health.

I was also delighted to learn that in France footpaths and bridlepaths are, to all intents and purposes, the same, and France is superbly served by them. Not only does each region have a network of local trails through the more attractive sections of countryside, but there are also long-distance routes spanning the whole country from end to end. These 'Sentiers de Grande Randonnée' (GR) are well-marked with red and white paint marks on trees, stones and fence-posts, almost invisible to the uninitiated, but invaluable to walkers and riders. No single path followed the whole of our chosen route to Brittany, but many sections went our way for a while and in the end more than half our time was spent on them. One surprising insight into the French character was revealed by the fact that, although we travelled in August and September, at the end of the holiday season, and although the paint was often fresh we hardly ever saw another traveller, mounted or on foot, using them for the purpose they were intended. Perhaps a dozen walkers in 1000 miles. The French seem to be past-masters at creating an infrastructure for certain activities, which practically no one then pursues. Fishing and shooting are another matter, but more on that later.

Originally, Louella and I had thought we would simply buy our two horses and perhaps a third as a pack animal to carry our tent, supplies and some corn for all three animals, and that we would ride in a leisurely way across autumnal France camping or stabling the horses while we slept in inns. Two things conspired to change this plan and on the whole for the better. It would be quite possible and in many ways extremely pleasant to be completely self-contained and I would certainly re-commend it to the traveller by horse who simply wants to see a part of France in an idyllic way. In fact I sincerely hope that this book may encourage others to do just that. I did not know before setting out how easy and delightful it would all be. But in our case there was a difference. While pleasure played a large part, the prime object was to get our two horses home as gently and with the least trouble as possible. And Camargue horses do not like being in stables. It was one of the first things we were told by the experts.

'Never put these horses indoors and never feed them unless the weather is really bad,' they said repeatedly. 'Camargue horses are used to living rough and being worked hard. You will ruin them if you mollycoddle them.'

Of course nothing could have pleased me more as these were precisely the qualities I was looking for, but I began to worry about the logistics of where we would stay each night. Finding a field would take longer than simply taking a stable attached to an inn, even if such establishments still existed, and I dreaded the prospect of frantic evenings spent search-ing for accommodation, perhaps followed, if unsuccessful, by ghastly nights sitting out in the pouring rain holding two horses as they grazed on wasteland next to a main road.

The second factor which I had not taken into account was the attraction our journey had for the media. My publishers suggested that I should write a book about it. The advance paid for the horses and the basic transport cost. Then the *Telegraph Sunday Magazine* bought the rights for a colour supplement, and it suddenly looked as if I would be in profit from the whole exercise. This had never been my intention, since Louella and I viewed the journey as a romantic idyll during which we could amble quietly across France enjoying the experience to the full. To be greedy would spoil the effect. However, suddenly we could afford to make the journey unashamedly sybaritic. If we had a ground crew driving an escort vehicle and arranging the horses' field as well as our evening's accommodation, we would be free to bask in the sheer enjoyment of what we were doing. Jamie Macpherson, the son of Scottish friends, had just left Fettes and was about to go to Aberdeen University. He could drive, ride, and speak French; he leapt at the chance of an all-expenses-paid holiday in France. Rupert, my about-to-be-14-year-old son, came as his assistant, to be replaced after a month when he went back to school by Jamie's girlfriend Alex.

Later still, the BBC suggested that they should make a film of the journey, as the director Howard Perks had become a good friend when we had made another film together during the summer. Once again we were at first doubtful, saying we did not want *paparazzi* watching our every move. Then inevitably the idea began to appeal, if only because we would have a really good home movie as a memento. Restricting them firmly to filming the beginning and end of the journey, with two brief visits en route we felt we would not be too distracted by the film crew. In fact we came to look forward to their arrival, bringing letters and news from home, as well as creating exciting interviews when for a moment we were stars.

It was Maggie who found us the horses. Shortly before John died in 1980 they had sold their own herd to their friend Jean-François Turquay.

'Your main problem with Jean-François,' said Maggie, 'will be getting him to accept your money. *Gardians* are intensely proud and honest. Once he says he will help you he will be completely committed to your best interests.'

We went to call on Jean-François and his attractive wife Rosalie shortly after our first meeting with Maggie in August 1983 and sat drinking *pastis* in their kitchen. I felt immediately that I could trust them. A burly working farmer with black hair and a ready smile, he accepted the role of intermediary without hesitation, saying that he would find us horses and have them ready to ride to England by the next summer. When I returned on my own the following April, he had still not been successful and I had a moment of doubt. But he mounted me on his own beautiful 11-year-old stallion and let me canter round and round the small private bullring in his farmyard. Sitting in John Skeaping's own saddle, which Maggie liked to see being used on the farm, I felt for the first time the true sensation of Camargue riding.

On our first visit Louella and I had gone as tourists on one of the innumerable *promenades à cheval* which line the main roads in the Camargue. Rows of bored white geldings stand tethered to the rail, their heads hanging in the sunshine, the flies clustered on their faces, as they wait for strangers to be placed on them. Often these are fat German housewives in shorts or giggling teenagers in bikinis who have never ridden before in their lives. One of our party was a little girl of three who was lashed to the saddle on which she perched like a trussed chicken. To our surprise the ride was rather fun. Although our mounts had stuck firmly to their appointed places in the line and refused to deviate from the regular programme, we were able to see and feel at first-hand what riding through that strange countryside might be like. We rode into the sea, forded a shallow river and even cantered through a marsh between the reed beds. All we had to do was sit there and enjoy it. The hour-long tour was led by a cantankerous old *gardian* who swore violently at anyone who stepped out of line and made it abundantly clear that he despised the lot of us. I enjoyed the final gallop and even managed to urge my horse to show a little spirit, although I felt awkward sitting low in the western saddle and bouncing uncomfortably against the unfamiliar pommel. Stimulated, I careered into the corral, only to be put firmly into my place by the old man, who said, *'Tu n'as pas aucune idée monter à cheval. Tu es comme un sac de patates.'*

Riding on Jean-François's stallion made me even more aware how much I had to learn about this form of horsemanship. My very first two actions landed me in trouble. Aware that I was sitting on a superb and highly charged animal, I gathered up the reins and gripped firmly with my knees. Immediately he took off at high speed round the ring, his feet thundering like a drum roll, head stretched forward, mane and tail flying.

'Drop the reins and sit back!' shouted Maggie, and when I did he stopped dead. It was all quite different from what I was used to at home, where my tough old horses with their hard mouths had to be yanked from side to side to make them turn and it took all our strength to stop them. Now I realised I had absolute control with the reins held gently between finger and thumb. Merely moving them from side to side across the neck made him turn sharply, a quick pull made him stop so suddenly he reared up on his hind legs, while laying the reins down on his neck and relaxing made him stop. Gently increasing the pressure of my knees caused controlled acceleration, and sitting well back in the saddle instead of leaning forward as I was used to doing was wonderfully comfortable.

Jean-François said he would find me the right horse in time, never fear. Meanwhile another friend of Maggie's had tracked down one which sounded ideal for Louella. As we hoped to use our horses for the rest of their lives on our farm in Cornwall, we wanted to buy them as young as possible. On the other hand, they had to be strong enough to stand the journey and Camargue horses are not fully grown until they are seven years old. This one was only four years old, but said to be exceptionally sturdy and gallant. It is only at about the age of four that Camargue horses, which are always born black or brown, turn white, and his legs were still grey. But he had a charming eye, strong bones, and a most endearing and affectionate nature. Everyone assured me that he would easily reach England and after a short trial ride I agreed to buy him for 7000 francs (about £585). First, however, he had to be castrated and this had already been arranged for the next morning. Only a few of the finest stallions are kept entire. Most of these live with the mares, who run wild in small herds and are never broken. The rest are gelded and become the riding horses used for searching the wide-open spaces of the Camargue for lost animals and for rounding up the bulls which also live wild. To have tried to have taken stallions home would have raised endless problems, not least those which would have cropped up each time we passed a field with a mare in it. Besides, we never wanted to breed Camargue horses, only to use them in Cornwall for a very similar purpose to that for which they had been developed over the years.

The castration turned out to be a ritual event which started at dawn and lasted for much of the morning. I was one of about a dozen men present at a smart suburban house where another horse was also due to be castrated. The owner greeted us with tumblers of wine as the sun rose and we stood in the paddock chatting nervously as both horses were injected with a powerful sedative. Leaving them while the drug took effect, we returned to the house where a feast had been prepared. Grilling on the red coals of a huge outdoor barbecue were hot spicy sausages; there was also bread, cheese and an enormous home-cured ham which was carved with much ceremony; wine was quaffed like lemonade. No women were seen throughout. The jokes became bawdy as nerves were calmed before an operation which clearly filled the men with a superstitious dread. The sense of occasion made it a rite of spring, the spilt wine a libation to the ancient Gods of Fertility.

Then, all at once, on with the job. The surgeon was a gypsy, young and good-looking, deferred to in all things, an expert at his trade. He also charged about ten per cent of the fee the local vet would have demanded. Skilfully he prepared his equipment. Four pairs of carved wooden clamps like giant clothes' pegs were thickly spread with a paste containing copper sulphate. Razor blades were unwrapped from greaseproof paper. Cloths, a bucket of water and an aerosol of purple spray were laid out neatly on the ground. The horses were now half asleep, their heads hanging down. Ropes were attached to each leg and Louella's horse was thrown on to his back. While one man sat on his head, the hind legs were pulled right forward and the operation was quickly performed. The wooden clamps were tied over the wounds as sutures, purple spray was liberally applied and a few minutes later the horse was up on his feet and I was walking him round the field.

Louella and I had decided that we would call our horses Thibert and Tiki: the first after Mas Thibert, the village where the finest Camargue saddles, including John Skeaping's, were and still are made; the second after the paddle steamer which plies the Petit Rhône to give tourists the best view of the great flocks of flamingos and the other wild life of the marshes. This was the moment I told Tiki his new name, whispering it into his ear as his senses gradually returned.

For a month he recuperated, then he was used during the summer as a lead horse on *promenades* where he could get fit and used to traffic. Jean-François searched the Camargue for a larger, stronger horse for me. All were agreed that one four-year-old was enough and that we would be pushing our luck if mine were not at least two years older and so better able to support both such a long journey and my extra weight. At last, a mere month before we were due to drive out, we heard that he had found one. One reason for the delay, I later learnt, was that he had rigorously refused to pay more than the 8000 francs we had discussed, although I would have been happy to do so. At the same time he was determined that the horse he found would, like Tiki, be a credit to the Camargue as they were to be the first two members of their breed to go to England.

During the April visit I had managed to find a perfect base for a two week holiday before we set off on the ride. Joining up with another family, the Woods, we were six adults and six children, far too many for the holiday flats and chalets along the coast. Almost all of these were booked for the start of the summer holidays anyway, and I was lucky to find enough room in a large working farm, the Mas de Pioch, nine kilometres inland from Les Saintes Maries-de-la-Mer. This put us in the very heart of the Camargue and, best of all, we could keep the horses there.

The day after we had all arrived and settled in, Thibert and Tiki were delivered. Thibert was indeed a fine horse, he sprang out of the box in a single leap and stood glaring round, his neck proudly arched. He was like a war horse, big and strong with a wide chest and massive shoulders. I blew into his nostrils and hoped it would not take too long for us to become friends.

Tiki arrived in a Citröen van which did not look large enough to take a donkey. He had cut his nose on the side so that when he stepped delicately out his lip was dripping blood. But he was as gentle and loving as I remembered, and Louella's three-year-old son Peter, who is mad about horses, was soon sitting bareback on him. We introduced the horses to each other and then turned them loose in a two-hectare field next to the farm where there was plenty of coarse grass. There they quickly became inseparable, standing or lying side by side at all times. One of the first and most attractive of their characteristics, which we learnt the next day, was that they would always come when we called them. Most of the horses I have had have been difficult to catch, which can be very irritating. With Thibert and Tiki we only had to appear at the gate and as soon as they saw us they would hurry over. We made a point of always having some feed, or at least an apple, carrot, or lump of sugar with us to greet them so as to encourage this trait, but it was hardly necessary as they seemed to have a genuine interest in the human race and to like people.

For the next two weeks we and the horses got to know each other. While the children and the rest of our party bathed in the sea, had picnics and visited some of the marvellous medieval walled towns and churches of the region, we started a regime of grooming, exercising and taking progressively longer rides together. We felt it was important to spend as much time as possible handling the horses; and so, rather to their initial surprise, as Camargue horses tend to be treated rough and are expected to fend for themselves, Thibert and Tiki found themselves being fussed over like show jumpers. We washed them down each day to remove the red dust which had been blown across the Mediterranean from North Africa on the sirocco. We anointed their minor cuts and chafes with creams and antiseptic spray. We fed them titbits. In no time at all they were following us around like dogs.

They lay down to sleep at night and sometimes, when we went to see how they were in the early morning, we could lie down beside them. Instead of leaping noisily to their feet like every other horse I have ever known, they would let us put our arms around their heads and cuddle them while the sun rose and began to warm us.

As we saddled up for our first ride everything was new and strange. We fumbled with unfamiliar harness and worried about fitting it together wrong, causing sores or making the horses uncomfortable. Our main fear was that through ignorance we would do something stupid and jeopardise the journey ahead. Maggie Skeaping had generously lent me John's saddle, which we already knew fitted both my horse and me, as I had ridden in it at Jean-François's farm, and Thibert had been worked in it there during the previous month. It was the most comfortable saddle imaginable, being designed and built with consummate skill, a work of art in every way. We were able to visit the workshop at Mas Thibert where it had been made by the late Jean Mison, whose saddles are now collectors' items, appreciating in value every year and worth more than the horses on which they are placed. His cousin Fernand Meffre carries on the trade to the same high standard. He told us proudly that when M. Mitterand paid a state visit recently to the USA he took as his present for President Reagan a Meffre saddle as representing the finest craftsmanship in France.

I had to learn a whole series of new knots and systems for saddling up. Instead of buckles on the girth, Camargue saddles have two thin leather thongs which are tied in such a way that they can be released instantly if the horse falls into one of the endless, and often bottomless, bogs. A third thong attaches the surcingle, which passes over the top of the saddle. Instead of a head collar every horse has a rope called a *seden* tied round its neck and so that this can be pulled hard without throttling him in such an emergency the knot used is a bowline. This is one of the best known climbers' and sailors' knots, which to my shame I had to relearn. The other end of the rope is neatly coiled and tied to the front of the saddle. Our *sedens*, which Maggie had ordered specially for us, were made of woven horsehair of three different colours.

Louella was to ride in a bullfighter's saddle which I had bought in a rash moment twenty years before in Portugal and had hardly used. The design was broadly similar to a Camargue saddle, and it was very pretty, being covered in soft blue suede decorated with many silver studs. Most important, it was much lighter, which was good for Tiki as he had not grown as much as we had hoped during the summer and was noticeably smaller than Thibert. It was not as comfortable as my saddle even with a soft leather cover which a friend of Louella's had brought back from the Argentine and lent her. But she never complained and most of the time I was allowed to forget how much better off I was.

The traditional Camargue stirrup is a most unusual sort of rounded metal cage in which the foot rests. It looks more appropriate for a knight in armour than a cowboy, but we found them very comfortable over long distances and useful when pushing through bushes on overgrown tracks. They are always hooked up to the back of the saddle when not being used. We commissioned M. Meffre to make special straps and attach them to Louella's saddle so that she too was properly turned out in the Camargue manner and was using at least some of his saddlery. At the same time he overhauled and restuffed John Skeaping's saddle for me.

We both wore chaps for the first time. Louella's came from Australia, brought back by her aunt Liz Hardy, who had been a great horsewoman there for many years. Mine were bought at the Royal Cornwall Show. Although we felt foolish at first, as though we were playing in some Wild West pantomime, they proved invaluable, preventing any rubs or blisters throughout. Moleskin trousers, short boots, check shirts and cheap but serviceable black *gardian* hats completed our outfits. I also bought a set of canvas saddlebags in which we carried wet-weather gear, cameras, maps and some biscuits or sweets.

At last we were ready to find out how the four of us were going to get on together. Shy of our awkwardness and inexperience in a region where horses were still used and understood by almost everyone, we waited until the farmyard was empty, then quietly mounted and walked out into the Camargue countryside.

2

The Camargue

The Camargue is very flat near the coast and distances are deceptive. Criss-crossed with innumerable canals and rivers hidden by dense reed beds, it is surprisingly easy to get lost there. An occasional clump of trees may seem to provide a bearing for a time, but necessary changes of direction to avoid lagoons or cultivated land alter the silhouette. Promising tracks turn out to lead only to an isolated field from which there is no exit, and a lonely farmhouse which has been chosen as a destination often has a canal just before it stretching to the horizon in either direction without a single bridge. Flat country seems much bigger too without views or contours. A secluded patch of open ground quite close to a farm or road but cut off by tall rushes and taller tamarisk along an abandoned canal seems like another world where no sounds intrude except the screeching of cicadas and the hum of bees. We began, very tentatively and gently, to explore.

It was all tremendously exciting. We planned to spend most of every day with the horses for the next two months. How would it feel? Would it really be as much fun as it had sounded when we had described our plans to our friends? Would it hurt? The first nasty shock came when we followed the verge along a stretch of main road near the farm. Thibert shied smartly out into the road every time we passed a white stone marker, dustbin or flapping metal signpost. Far from slowing down when they see horses ahead, most French drivers seem to accelerate, roaring past as fast and as close as possible, sometimes with a toot on the horn or a shout from the open window to add to the fun. Sooner or later it seemed inevitable that Thibert would sidestep into a car and that would be the end of our journey. The odds against our arriving undamaged in England looked at that stage overwhelming.

Tiki, though much younger, was much more sensible. Both he and Louella took the traffic and the other dangers in their stride, leading the way for Thibert and me, who were much more neurotic whenever potential problems loomed. These became known to us as Thibert's lions, as he clearly suspected everything unfamiliar to be a lion in disguise, just waiting to jump out at him. We gradually developed an instinct for spotting lions before he did.

Once off the road, however, lions were fewer and we could begin to relax and enjoy our surroundings. There is a kind of hum all over the Camargue. The sky is so big and the land stretches away so far in all directions that sounds are flattened and seem to come from everywhere at once. Wind, distant traffic, seagulls, human voices, insects, blur into a background harmony. Only the sudden plop of a fish jumping or the clatter of a bird taking off disturbed the immediate silence, making Thibert jump. We rode past fields of asparagus and corn; past the neat straight rows of the low vines growing on bare sand, which produce the quite popular local 'Vin de Sable'; past wet rice paddies, where the sky was reflected, startling blue round the bright green shoots. Then, on poorer uncultivated land we passed herds of white horses grazing patiently, their long tails constantly swishing to remove troublesome flies and clegs which swarmed by day, sometimes so numerous that they would turn a white head black. In the evening the same effect could be produced by the mosquitoes which hid for the most part during the heat of the day to re-emerge in late afternoon and hunt man and beast greedily throughout the night. At the side of each mare frisked a delightful black or brown foal. With his short tufted mane and ineffectual little tail he stood motionless next to his mother for a while, then gave a sudden leap high in the air – whether because of a particularly sharp bite or out of sheer exuberance was hard to tell. Then he stared at us with interest as we rode past, the white blaze on his forehead extending round his eyes to give him a surprised look.

In the wet swamps and open lagoons birds swarmed. Great flocks of seagulls settled on the water, long legged white storks patrolled in their stately way in the deeper parts. Black-winged stilts, now formed into large groups before flying off to Africa, carefully placed their long red legs one after the other in their constant search for food. Innumerable smaller waders worked over the shallows. The finest sight of all in the Camargue, and one which always gave me a moment's doubletake at coming across something so exotically incongruous on the mainland of Europe, was provided by the flamingos. The year before, when we had gone for an evening's cruise up the Petit Rhône in the *Tiki*, we had been lucky enough to see a formation of two hundred flamingos fly over our heads into the setting sun. It was a scene straight from a wildlife documentary film which did not tempt us to try and photograph it but rather to gaze in amazement and delight as one after the other the extraordinary birds streamed past, their necks stretched way out in front, their long legs trailing straight behind. Now we could ride quite close to them as they fed in smaller groups, stepping delicately in water barely three inches deep as they scooped up food with their strong, strangely shaped bills. Pink and white they looked until they flapped their wings revealing a flash of bright scarlet, the sort of healthy colour seldom seen in zoos or bird parks.

On drier land there were hoopoes calling, fluttering past like giant butterflies or glimpsed feeding on the ground. Seeing a hoopoe in France once with my mother when she took me as a child on a walking holiday in the Alpes Maritime is one of my most vivid early memories. I have seen only a few since, but the Camargue was full of them and they seemed as common as jays are at home.

It was a good place to spend our summer holidays. The children mixed well and found important business around the farm and at the seaside. There were some willows outside the cottage where we and some of our party slept, and between these we slung my Brazilian hammock in which hot afternoons were lazed away. On a patch of grass below, Rupert and Alexander, the eldest of the Wood boys, shared the tent we planned to use from time to time on the ride. Harry, Louella's elder boy, and Henry Wood, spent hours collecting frogs, toads, tadpoles and fish from the canals and irrigation ditches which intersected the farm. The mosquitoes were bad at times and everyone was bitten, three-year-old Peter so badly that it looked as though the chickenpox with which he had arrived had never cleared up. But it was a pleasant and friendly place and I think everyone agreed that it was much more fun and interesting than a holiday flat on the coast.

I felt a bit stiff after the first couple of days' riding in an unfamiliar saddle and thought I had better make myself fitter for the ride ahead. Going for a run before breakfast was the answer. Although I have never taken jogging seriously there are few greater pleasures than running for a few miles in the dawn to arrive back feeling wonderful when everyone else is getting up. Then we would bring the horses in to feed and groom them under the trees while the children made ready for the beach. John Perkins, the *Sunday Telegraph* photographer, arrived to cover our departure. Equipped with devastating good looks and irresistible charm he is great fun to work with. As he dashes about, his heavy camera gear slung over his shoulder in a battered canvas bag, he has the ability to make everyone do just what he wants. Farmers down tools and pose for him, little old ladies pick up their knitting for him, girls giggle and try to look their prettiest. John made us saddle up and unsaddle for him, which was good practice anyway as well as posing and riding hand in hand against suitable backdrops. Once he asked me to ride back to the farm and fetch a light meter he had left behind. Louella stayed with him but Tiki suddenly objected to being separated from his new friend and reared high on his hind legs. When he was just about to fall over backwards Louella dropped off, landing heavily on her back. When she had calmed him down and climbed stiffly back into the saddle she asked John if he had at least caught a good picture of the incident which, she felt, must have looked pretty dramatic. John, thinking this was normal horse behaviour and nothing out of the ordinary, said the light had been wrong and would she like to do it again.

As we and the horses enjoyed the magic of the Camargue we began to stretch ourselves a bit more, riding morning and evening for up to two or three hours. The horses were beginning to walk out well together now, although Thibert's stride was longer than Tiki's, so that I would keep forging ahead and Louella had to canter to catch up. This remained a constant problem as trotting was uncomfortable and generally to be avoided in those saddles. Tiki surprisingly cantered faster than Thibert and we started to enjoy ourselves thundering along side by side, although we were beginning to be worried by a nasty cough which he had had from the day of his arrival and which seemed to be getting worse. Going farther afield was fun and we were able to start calling on some of the friends we had made round about. One of these was a young Englishwoman called Brenda who ran one of the better riding establishments. Patiently she had instructed us in the finer points of riding à la Camargue, including how to use a Cavesson bridle so as to continue training our horses to respond to neck reining. We were relieved when she said that both Thibert and Tiki should survive the journey to England and were good buys.

Another emigrée was Vivien Wilson, who rather surprisingly bred beautiful Palomino stallions at a farm not far from ours. She had a large open-air lunch party a week after we arrived and to which we were invited. We thought it would be fun to ride over in our full travelling gear as a rehearsal for the start and we arrived feeling rather dashing. Predictably, disaster struck. We unsaddled and took our places at the long table set for 32, the scent of a whole lamb being barbecued nearby drifting over us and honing our appetites. Brenda was another guest and we mentioned that we were a bit worried about Tiki's health. He was coughing more, his breathing seemed laboured when cantering and he lacked vigour. She diagnosed *gourme* (strangles) immediately. Said it was highly contagious and that for the sake of Vivien's horses we should leave at once. She did not even want to go near our mounts herself as she might then carry the infection to her own horses, which would mean that she would have to cease business for at least three weeks. We rode home worried and hungry, to return later and share what was left of the excellent feast.

When the vet arrived he was reassuring. Yes, it was *la gourme* all right but that was quite common in the Camargue unlike in England, where strangles has a reputation for being fatal. The course of penicillin injections I had already started to give him was the correct treatment and he should recover in a few days. In fact it was just as well he had caught the disease, as he would now have some immunity against it and should not catch it again on our way across France. Best of all, he said that we could leave as planned at the end of the week. But we must not ride Tiki any more before then. Moreover Thibert would probably catch it too and I should be ready to give him a course of injections as well at the first sign of trouble.

We were now able to spend more time with the children and explore the region. We all went to the remarkable ancient town of Les Baux, perched on an escarpment overlooking the Rhône delta. From the vertiginous edge of the cliff we could see the smoking factories of Marseilles far to our left; the Camargue marshes and, faintly, the church steeple of Les Saintes Maries-de-la-Mer with the sea beyond and Thibert and Tiki invisible grazing somewhere in front; and away to the right the foothills of the Cevennes through which we would be riding. It all looked a very long way from that height.

Before leaving home I had written to all the equestrian societies along our route asking for advice on footpaths and bridle paths. Through the President of the Association Régionale de Tourisme Equestre of Provence, M. Roque, known as 'l'Homme à Cheval', I learned that we were in luck. The one man who could give us accurate and up-to-date information on the first 200 miles of our journey had just arrived at the coast, having ridden down from Figéac in Perigord. His name was Paul Nayrolle and I found him camped with his horses in a pine wood near Le Grau-du-Roi. A wiry man with grey hair, blue eyes, blue jeans and jacket, he looked like a gypsy, his face nut-brown from wind and weather. In a strong wind we laid out maps, anchoring them with stones on the sand beneath the trees and Paul carefully marked the route, giving a fast running commentary about difficulties and facilities we would meet on the way. I scribbled furiously as he told me.

'Here the mayor is friendly and he will let you put the horses in the bull ring. This place has no shops or café; you will need to bring your own food. Look out for any chance to water the horses on this stretch and let them drink well; there are not many springs. Here is the telephone number of my friend Daniel, the blacksmith. He will come to you wherever you are when you need him. Don't worry about finding the way. I have paint-marked it myself and you cannot get lost!'

It was an invaluable meeting, hugely reassuring. The only slight worry was the schedule we had set ourselves. Paul, with a string of 12 horses and some inexperienced riders, had taken 16 days to cover the route. We hoped to do it in 10. He said it would be a close thing.

Back with the children, we bathed in the sea, making sandcastles and catching crabs on the long beach stretching away to the east of Les Saintes Maries-de-la-Mer, where the further we were prepared to drive along the very rough track, the fewer the crowds of tourists, who packed the beaches in the centre of the town at this the height of the French holiday season.

And we went on another *promenade à cheval*. This was an important and interesting ride which we had hoped to do on Thibert and Tiki. Instead we hired some of the usual obstinate, bored nags and rode through the *pinède* to the sea. John Perkins came with us to photograph us riding in the waters of the Mediterranean and so did Rupert and several members of the Wood family. We were also joined by Philip Purser who had been sent out by the *Telegraph Sunday Magazine* to cover our story and who had never sat on a horse before. He felt he should experience at first hand what we were in for and with great courage and good humour endured uncomplainingly a most uncomfortable time. Before we had been going an hour I could see that his backside had been rubbed raw and blood was seeping through his trousers.

The *pinède* is a wonderfully wild and unspoilt bit of the Camargue from which tourists are banned except for those on horses like ourselves. Instead of the flat open country we had become used to, we found ourselves in extensive pine forests growing on sand dunes. It was a romantic, hidden landscape culminating in a spectacular view of the sea across a wide-open stretch of sand where we could gallop down to the water's edge and pose pointing optimistically inland towards England.

Louella and I also had time to visit the famous biological station at Tour du Valat. In 1950 Luc Hoffmann bought 5000 acres in one of the most remote and undisturbed parts of the Camargue. He originally acquired it as a shooting estate since tens of thousands of migratory duck settle there in the winter. However, the scientific interest of the place soon conquered the sporting attraction and today it is one of the most important centres for wetland research in the world. A whole host of subjects is studied by more than forty scientists who produce a constant stream of learned papers on the valuable and fragile ecosystem. Our particular interest lay in seeing their herd of truly wild Camargue horses. The way in which Camargue horses usually run free does not mean that they are behaving as wild horses would. Their stallions are selected for them by the farmer who also removes their male offspring, feeds them and keeps them enclosed, albeit in a fairly large area. Since horses no longer exist in the wild and so cannot be studied in their natural state, it was a fascinating plan to create a wild herd at Tour du Valat, which would be left strictly alone to see what happened. This was done in 1973 and we would see the result.

We met Luc Hoffmann, who was charming and courteous but just leaving for a conference in Madagascar. He handed us over to Patrick Duncan, a friend with whom we had already corresponded, who was in charge – among his other responsibilities – of the horse programme. He showed us on the map the extent of the area over which the horses grazed and the different habitats they preferred, ranging from reed beds and salt flats to better pasture. Originally there were seven mares with six offspring and one stallion. By 1980 this number, through a strict policy of non-interference, had increased to ninety. They had been given no supplementary feed or veterinary treatment, yet their numbers had increased much more than expected, or would have probably happened with, for example, deer or cattle. Of course they had no predators as would have been the case were they really facing nature as horses must have done throughout their evolution, when the sabre-toothed tiger roamed Europe. But the ways in which they had been found to avoid inbreeding and break up into small family groups rather than one large herd were the subjects of many fascinating scientific papers.

When we set out to look for the horses we could not at first find them, as they were not where Patrick, with his long and intimate knowledge of them, expected them to be. Then we saw them out in the middle of a bare open salt flat and we stopped the car to get out and walk towards them. We were told that, having never been handled or bothered by man for ten years, yet used to the almost constant presence of people, they would ignore us. Patrick had said firmly that we should on no account do anything to disturb the horses and above all we must resist the temptation to reach out and stroke the foals if any came up to us.

Walking among those beautiful wild horses was one of the most spellbinding experiences of my life. They did indeed ignore us, the mares only glancing up as we strolled between them and their foals. One or two of these did approach us and Patrick muttered crossly that some Americans were suspected of having recently petted them. For the rest we might have been invisible. Many horses I have known have tended to pretend maddeningly that they were deeply interested in some object in the distance over my shoulder, when I knew well that if I took one step closer to catch them they would take off at top speed. Others, like Thibert and Tiki, are all too keen to see what I have in my pockets. It was a distinctly odd and rather salutary sensation to realise that for these horses I virtually did not exist and their interest in other things was genuine. We were even able to talk without disturbing them and Patrick began to point out the relationship between the different groups and their members. At first they had just looked like an amorphous herd of horses of all ages and sizes, but as he explained what was going on we were able to see how each family kept itself just a bit apart from the others. As they moved across the plain the pattern blurred and reformed constantly, but once understood it never changed. Each horse was in a dynamic relationship with all the rest.

Most of the groups consisted of one or two mares with their foals, a few young, a boss stallion and often a substitute stallion, who appeared to accept his subordinate role equably. But in fact every member of the group is alert to the possibility of change, and constantly has an eye to the main chance. The stallion, of course, is always on the lookout for any other male straying too close to his mares. We saw one young filly quite deliberately wander off towards the handsome boss of the next group and get firmly nipped back into line for her trouble. The foals were constantly in some sort of potential mischief. Two of the stallions on the outskirts of the herd had a practice fight rearing up on their hindlegs snapping at each other.

Stupid people sometimes say that life must be dull for wild animals. The tribal peoples, with whom I have spent so much time in different parts of the world, are often accused of spending lives that are nasty, brutish and short. I began to see a parallel between the two prejudices, which fail to recognise the zest for life, the constant interest of every moment, the healthy and proper dynamic of cause and effect in an interesting and vibrant world working according to accepted natural and traditional laws. The lives of domestic animals, cows in their field, hens in their houses may well be dull. Doubtless the psychological vacuum of their empty lives makes them look half-alive next to their wild cousins. In just the same way an urbanised, sedentary, overcrowded life makes most modern human beings into a physical and psychological mess.

The Yanomami Indians of Brazil, a tribe with whom I spent three months in 1980 in the company of a French anthropologist, were thought to be uncontrollably fierce and violent until further research revealed it was all a cultural device to avoid conflict. They too live in a constant state of dynamic interaction with their families and neighbours and they are the first to assert that their lives are the richest imaginable.

Being in the company of such a stimulating scientist as Patrick Duncan inspired me to pursue this wild comparison as we watched the herd wander off towards the marshes to drink. We felt hugely privileged to have been allowed to spend some time with them, and our affection for Camargue horses in general became even stronger.

If you read some of the lavishly illustrated guide books to the Camargue, you will learn that the white horses of the region are the scarcely modified descendants of the original wild horses which populated prehistoric Gaul and are reproduced in cave paintings at Lascaux and elsewhere. Others will tell you that they are of North African origin, having Barb and Arab blood and it has even been suggested that they were introduced from Tibet or Chinese Turkestan. It would be nice to think that these romantic herds of half wild horses have lived in the same desolate region of France breeding pure for thousands of years. Certainly there have been famous horses there for a very long time. There is a letter dated AD 399 from the prefect of Rome to a friend of his farming in the Camargue asking him to supply some sturdy steeds to be raced in one of the circuses. In more recent centuries the fortunes of horsebreeders have fluctuated with European wars during which there was often a good demand for strong cavalry mounts.

The findings of some preliminary research by Tour du Valat scientists have, however, shown that Camargue horses are a complete mix. Arab and wild blood seems to have contributed rather little to their make-up, but they are clearly not a race apart, lying somewhere between thorough-breds and pony breeds in the diversity of their genetic make-up. But they have lived for an exceptionally long time in the wetlands of the Rhône delta and they have adapted in remarkable ways to the harsh conditions to be found there, becoming exceptionally hardy and resilient. They have been bred selectively for their intelligence and skill at working with cattle and coping with difficult and dangerous terrain. Best of all they are universally recognised as having particularly nice natures so that they will respond to their names being called at a great distance and approach their master.

The list of official features recognised in the perfect Camargue horse (see Appendix 3) concludes: sensible, lively, agile, brave, and with great stamina, the Camargue horse can withstand long fasts, endure bad weather and complete long journeys.

Some of these characteristics we were beginning to recognise and appreciate in Thibert and Tiki. Now the time had come to leave and we would find out if they possessed the rest or if we were, after all, asking too much of them.

3

En Route via Bulls

We left the Mas de Pioch on the morning of Friday 10 August. As we caught, fed, groomed and saddled up our horses, our every move was filmed. Howard Perks, the BBC director from Plymouth, had arrived with his assistant the day before. That morning they teamed up with the French film crew supplied by FR3, a French television network company, with whom they had a joint contract. Since neither side spoke a word of the other's language, I was the interpreter. This added to the already strong sense of unreality as we waited for the clapperboard to clap before undertaking each operation or repeated them so that they could be caught from a better angle. The tensions of the past fortnight had been building to this climax, the anxieties about the health of the horses and the task we were setting them, the sadness inevitable at the end of a happy family holiday (particularly for Louella who was to part from her two little boys until we returned to Cornwall) and our eagerness to be off all conspired to make the delays almost unbearable. Normally I like to say Goodbye and leave quickly, but that was not possible as it was an important moment which had to be properly recorded. The children acted well, running across to kiss us. Peter trotted over to Tiki and reached up to kiss his tummy. Rupert, who was coming with us for the first month, nonetheless made a great show of hugging his stepmother. We leapt into our saddles and rode off waving . . . only to be called back to do it all again.

Then we were quite suddenly alone and riding from the end of the farm track across country on what was inescapably the start of our journey home through France. Thibert and Tiki, having not been ridden for some days, were quite frisky, unaware that they were leaving their native soil for ever. A bee-eater, its vivid blue and yellow, green and russet plumage giving the day a splash of colour, flew right round us as it darted about catching insects in the air. A good omen, we thought.

For four wide fields, past vines and asparagus, through a dense reed bed where the mosquitoes lay in wait, we allowed the thrill of being really on our way to roll over us. We held hands and revelled in the moment. Then there was the camera ahead again and would we mind moving out into the edge of a flooded paddy field and cantering so as to give a good splash effect?

Soon after, we were facing our first serious hazard, one which would test all our nerves fully. The only way out of the Camargue to the west involved crossing the iron bridge across the Petit Rhône at Sylvéréal. A noisy, narrow affair caged in by alarming girders and with a sheer drop to the river some way below, the traffic raced across it with an almost constant roar. Thibert and I were very nervous and worried at the prospect, but with our car coming behind us with flashing lights and the film crew stopping anyone approaching, we rode side by side towards the cameras and came safely over. Without waiting for a retake to be suggested, we cantered off to the left along the Canal de Peccais. The towpath was deeply rutted and unsuitable for vehicles so that we were safe from pursuit or *paparazzi* for the next hour or so.

After the blazing sun and dry wind of the last two weeks, we had enjoyed a grey morning following a little rain in the night which had laid the dust. Everyone had assured us that the day would improve. Foolishly I had believed them and with some misguided idea that it would lighten his load, I had not bothered to pack our waterproof capes in Thibert's saddlebags. Half-way along the canal the skies opened and we were soaked to the skin by icy rain. My mood of euphoria instantly changed and Louella was treated to a display of extreme bad temper as I cursed and swore while the rain trickled down our necks. My only excuse for these bouts of insufferable behaviour is that they were always caused by my own incompetence, usually through reading the map wrong and getting us lost. The fury was directed at myself, but that did not mean that anyone within range was not likely to be sworn at as well. Louella has learned well how to deal with these moments when I regard myself as being in the grip of an impressive, towering rage, by dismissing them as 'tantrettes', short for little tantrums.

Poor Jamie had only arrived the evening before. He had come out by bus to Montpellier, which he had reached at five in the morning. Our arrangement had been that he would try to hitchhike and if unsuccessful would telephone me at the farm so that I could come and fetch him. Exhausted after 48 hours in a cramped seat, he had set off to find that absolutely no one would stop for him despite his most pleading expression. What he did not know – and nor did we until later – was that there had recently been a spate of very ugly murders in the South of France, the victims being drivers who had given people lifts. Jamie had tried to ring me time after time, but had failed to master the intricacies of the French telephone system and constantly heard only the unobtainable signal. We had found him at dusk after he had walked

ABOVE Thibert and Tiki meet for the first time at the Mos de Pioch.

LEFT Louella giving Thibert and Tiki their final feed before setting off from the Camargue.

BELOW Tiki's hind feet elegantly at rest.

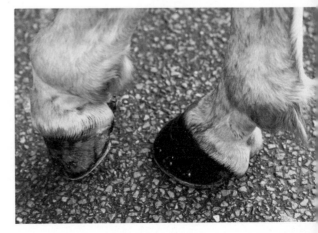

ABOVE LEFT Riding through the Pinède.

ABOVE John P. weighed down by his camera equipment.

LEFT Selecting the bulls at the *abrivado*.

OVERLEAF When things go wrong it can be dangerous. This time the horse was unhurt, but the man who fell broke his leg.

ABOVE A *razéteur* making a grab for the cockade. In French bullfighting the bulls are not hurt at all.

RIGHT Maggie Skeaping and Frank Fauvet seeing us off.

ABOVE Louella tacking up while Tiki 'saves his nervous energy for action'.

RIGHT The 11th-century apse at St Guilhem-le-Désert.

ABOVE RIGHT Saying goodnight after our long day's ride. The hammocks are slung between the car's roof-rack and a tree.

about 40 kilometres carrying his pack. I was quite unsympathetic, saying that he had earned no Brownie points for initiative yet.

Having skilfully found a route along farmtracks to a rendezvous point at a junction in the canal and perhaps expecting praise, he was greeted by me with a bad tempered expression of hope that he had not driven the car too fast over the ruts and a demand to lend me his Barbour raincoat. Luckily he had a sunny disposition which was almost impossible to ruffle and he was enjoying driving my large and expensive estate car too much to mind. I had woken him at dawn to take him for a quick test run in the car and reassured myself that he could drive, which was just as well as we were going to be totally dependent on his ability in this area for the next seven weeks. At just 18 it was, I realised, expecting quite a lot of him.

Rupert and Jamie had stopped beside a romantic, moated Vauban fort. Solid and uncompromising, its thick low walls and turrets stood alone in the middle of a huge flat landscape. As it was all of three miles inland from the coast, its function was presumably to guard the canal but it must have been a lonely posting when occupied. Rupert had managed to cross the moat and was happily exploring the interior so that he barely noticed us passing.

As we rode towards the impressive fortified walls of Aigue-Mortes, John Perkins and Philip Purser found us and guided us through the suburbs. John appeared, as usual, to have made friends with everyone already so that we innocently did as he told us, little realising that he was leading us into a trap which would, he hoped, produce a vivid picture epitomising a conflict of Anglo-French attitudes. First, we rode up to a group of old ladies sitting sewing outside their houses in the street. They were welcoming and friendly saying, between toothless grins that, had they known we were coming they would have prepared a feast for us. Then John, placing himself with his telephoto lens and tripod at the far end of a wide boulevard, directed us to ride down the sandy middle stretch where several elderly gentlemen were playing *boule*. It was a good smooth and soft surface which the horses enjoyed after the stretch of street and they stepped out proudly, scuffing up the ground as they pranced. A chorus of furious and unfamiliar expletives greeted us. For a moment I thought there must be some minor misunderstanding and attempted to explain in my best French that our photographer friend had arranged that we could ride across this patch of ground. Then I realised that we were in the middle of a carefully prepared, raked and rolled pitch on which a very serious game was being played. It was the equivalent of trotting across the Oval during a Test Match, and the fury was becoming homicidal.

We took off up a side street pursued by a fist-waving mob and hurried to lose ourselves in the crowds of tourists pouring into the town through one of the great gateways. Aigues-Mortes, which was originally built in 1248 as the embarkation point for the Seventh Crusade, has attractive narrow streets crisscrossing the town inside the still complete medieval fortifications. We rode along one of these, stopped for a policeman at an intersection, were waved on as though horses were fully expected in the town centre, and came out through another gateway into open space again. The south-eastern sides of Aigues-Mortes are even more spectacular in that the marshy flats (*aquae mortuae*) from which it was named come right up to the walls without a single house built outside to spoil the impression that one has stepped back in time. There we met our film crew again and contributed to the illusion ourselves by cantering along like troubadours under the ramparts – a single long panning shot in which nothing visible was modern or would have spoiled the continuity had we been filming *Camelot*.

It was still raining and we sheltered under a small postern gate where we were brought wine and long rolls of crusty bread and cheese by our faithful ground crew. They also dug out dry shirts for us from the luggage in the car and towels with which we could have a rub down. It all looked promising for the future, we thought, and we set off again for the second half of our first day full of enthusiasm and energy.

The next obstacle we faced after some pleasant riding along the towpath of the Canal du Midi, was a causeway across an area of swamp which we had already established could not be crossed in any other way. A busy highway with no verge ran along the raised road and we would be at the mercy of the traffic. In the middle was a high tower, the Tour Carbonnière, which used to guard Aigues-Mortes from attack from the land side. From the top of this John Perkins, leaning perilously out through the castellations, managed to get some dramatic pictures of us braving the dangers of French roads, while Jamie in the car held right back, his flashers and hand signals vainly urging drivers to slow down.

Once safely across, it was only a short way to the farm where we had arranged accommodation for the horses and the boys that night. This was owned by a friend of Maggie Skeaping's called Frank Fauvet. His daughter Anne and son-in-law lived in a comfortable house they had built on the farm and they welcomed us warmly. The horses were put in a lush pasture where they set to grazing hard to make up for lost time during the day. For some days we had been feeding them morning and evening half a bucket each of horse nuts, which we had bought from a neighbouring Camargue farm. In order to keep their strength up we continued this throughout the journey, encouraging them to eat their fill while we picked out and oiled their feet as well as grooming them and combing out their manes and tails. Their feet were, we felt, especially important and vulnerable in view of the excessive wear and work to which they were about to be subjected, and so we religiously rubbed special greases and unguents into every part of their hoofs in order to prevent cracks or splits developing.

M. Fauvet and his daughter were passionate *aficionados* of the local form of bullfighting, which was in full swing at this particular time of the year. For the month of August the handful of villages in this area hold a week long fête at which the bulls are run and contests are held each day. They were to take part in the gathering and running of the bulls into the nearby village of Le Cailar the next morning and insisted that we simply must take part too so that we should see something of what the Camargue was really all about. This spectacular traditional display is called the *abrivado* and it sounded exciting and fun. As the BBC team declared that it should provide just the dramatic sequence they were so far lacking we agreed to do it although we were slightly worried that we might risk injuring our horses and so ruin the journey before we had even left the Camargue. Little did we know what we were letting ourselves and them in for.

We gathered in a huge pasture where a herd of 200 bulls grazed peacefully out in the centre while horsemen, their mounts, friends and hangers-on created the atmosphere of a country fair. There were vans dispensing wine and food, groups around fires having substantial barbecue breakfasts, rows of cars, caravans and horseboxes – and at least 60 horses saddled and waiting for the *abrivado* to begin. There was a tense air of expectancy which disturbed us as we had only the vaguest idea of what was going to happen. But M. Fauvet and Anne were clearly in their element and eager for the fray. Thibert and Tiki, who had been brought from the field in M. Fauvet's horsebox, were excited and hard to control. They bucked and sidestepped, clearly longing to take off at full speed, while all we wanted to do was stay on the outskirts and watch what was going on.

At last a group consisting of most of the *gardians* cantered over to the herd of bulls and neatly cut out six. Surrounding them in a tight formation they attempted to gallop them once round the field in a wide circle. But one broke away and returned to the herd. At once they stopped to recapture the miscreant and drove him back into the chosen group. Three times this happened as the tension rose and we all careered round in what seemed to me an increasing state of disorganisation. Already, although it was all great fun, I was beginning to regret having come and told myself that we were fools to risk the whole enterprise in an activity in which the likelihood of a horse being kicked or injured in some other way seemed extremely high.

Then suddenly we were being shouted at and told to catch up with the others as this time they had got it together properly. It was an amazing, inspiring scene, quite unlike anything I had ever seen before and yet strangely familiar, from some folk memory perhaps. The whole mass of horses, with the bulls invisible buried somewhere in the centre, was moving as a single unit. Shoulder to shoulder they pranced proudly in unison gathering speed as they circled the field like a discus thrower as he turns to gather momentum. We joined on the end and found ourselves launched in a trajectory which took us all up on to the bank of the canal and off along the towpath. We literally thundered along, the dust of our hoofs rising around us, the faces of the clustered *gardians* fixed and ecstatic as they concentrated on their task. We began to be caught up in the spirit of the moment, though we still hung back at the tail of the group; it all began to be more enjoyable, although there was an excessive number of people on foot and even some battered old cars and motor bikes which struck a false note with us. What we did not know and had not been told was that at an *abrivado* it is traditional for the spectators to do everything in their power to disturb the proceedings, make the horses separate and so cause a bull to escape. Everyone who was not on a horse was therefore our enemy. We were amazed and not a little cross, when apparently disobeying all the normal rules of conduct some of the cars roared up the canal bank and tried to barge in amongst us. Full of wildly shouting teenagers covered in paint and brandishing flags and paper bags, they seemed manifestations of my worst nightmares of what might lie in wait for us on the French roads. When they began to throw the paper bags at the horses and these burst to release clouds of white flour, I knew that everyone had gone mad. One of the runners, in shorts and singlet, fell in front of the stampede and was trampled over by the whole mad rush. I glanced back to see him stagger to his feet, apparently unhurt and run to catch us up. When another ran up to us, grabbed Tiki's bridle and tried to pull Louella from her saddle, she felt that enough was enough and raised the silver headed stick her father had given her for the ride to beat him off. 'If she does that they will throw her in the canal,' said a voice at my elbow in French. Hurriedly translating for Louella's benefit and trying to help her as we hurtled along, I asked our neighbour if he came here often. He was riding a large bay and wearing conventional riding breeches which made him look distinctly odd among the white horses and *gardians* in their customary outfits who surrounded us. 'Oh yes, I come every year,' he replied. 'I am a film maker from Dijon and this is for me the most exciting sport in the world.'

What surprised us most about the whole experience, since we were totally unprepared for it, was the sense of violent enmity expressed by the whole world towards us as we rode. We really felt in grave danger from the horde who ran and drove alongside us throwing things and hurling abuse and it was quite frightening. Yet Anne up in front seemed to be enjoying herself hugely and M. Fauvet, who had left at the start to bring on the horsebox would, we were sure, never have let us get involved in anything really dangerous.

After about three miles we entered the outskirts of Le Cailar and at a small square stopped while the central core of *gardians* took the bulls on to the *toril*, the enclosure in the bull ring where the animals were to be kept before entering the arena. At once the atmosphere changed. As we dismounted, half expecting the mob to set on us and tear us limb from limb, we were surrounded by relaxed smiling faces who asked us how we had enjoyed ourselves and was it really true that we were taking these two horses all the way to England? By the look of Thibert and Tiki at that moment they would hardly have made it back to the Mas de Pioch. Their flanks were heaving and they were covered in sweat and mud, but we cheerfully assured everyone that we foresaw no problems as we rubbed them dry with a couple of old towels which Rupert and Jamie produced, having caught us up.

Everyone in the Camargue is an expert on horses and ours were looked over critically. We were pleased when several pundits agreed that Tiki was *'sur l'oeil'*, meaning that he had a strong character, and that Thibert had a *'bon pied'*, indicating that he would not fall.

Since there was now to be a gap of some hours before the contests in the afternoon, we loaded Thibert and Tiki into M. Fauvet's box so that they could return to their field. Meanwhile we took everyone else off for an open-air lunch in a neighbouring village, St Laurent d'Aigouze. There the bull ring is in the central square next to the church, which is used as the *toril* during their own festival a week later, so that the bulls are actually coralled in the aisle. There too we had discovered a particularly good small restaurant. Not yet in any of our guide books it was called the Table d'Oc and was owned and run by Jean-Pierre Clamel who had become a firm friend. Quite unmoved by the arrival of 12 unexpected guests and although, as I found out later, he did not normally do lunches on a Saturday, he cheerfully produced a delicious impromptu meal of salad and cold meats, followed by a superb *tarte*, for a derisory sum. At the end he insisted I accept a huge photograph on canvas which showed the dramatic moment during the running of the bulls through *his* village when a bull knocked to the ground and jumped over the *gardian* and his horse.

After lunch we all returned in good spirits to find the contest about to begin. The film crew had secured a good vantage-point and we scrambled over people to join them. It was a charming shaded bull ring, the tiers of benches built around and through the large plane trees of the square so that, although the view of what was going on was perfect for no one, the ambience was so ideal it was clear that no one minded. A trumpet fanfare announced the arrival of the *razéteurs*. All dressed in white shirts and trousers, about twenty young men leapt into the ring, vaulting over the barricade like acrobats. Some held in their right hands an object like a horse comb, the *crochet*, which is used to snatch the trophies from between the bull's horns. Others were empty handed and it was explained to us that their rôle was to act as decoys. Another fanfare announced the entry of the first bull. It charged into the ring with all the snorting and pawing of the sandy ground one could have wished for. The young men fell back a pace. The bull stormed across the plaza to worry the wooden barrier below us with its horns. We could see that a piece of string had been wound several times around each horn and stretched between them. From the base of the horns hung woollen tassels and in the centre was a small piece of red cloth, the *cocarde* (cockade), the most prized trophy.

A *razéteur* challenged the bull and when it turned to charge him, he ran ahead of it reaching back to grab for its *cocarde* so that it seemed inevitable that he would be gored by the sharp horns. At the very last possible moment he threw himself at the barricade and with one giant stride stepped on to the top and leaped beyond to cling to one of the uprights surrounding the ring. We could see how the name *razéteur* arose: these boys pass so close to the bull they literally shave it. This time the bull swerved away, but later several chose to continue their rush, themselves leaping over the barricade in their pursuit and landing in the walled passage between the inner and outer rings. This was then rapidly cleared as the bull charged around it until released once more into the arena.

A female announcer kept up a running commentary using many Provençal patois words which made it hard to understand exactly what was going on, but we soon had the general idea and were cheering with the rest. Each successful snatch earned a cash prize and I persuaded Howard Perks that the least the BBC could do was contribute a small sum to acknowledge the courage of the young men we were filming. He and I both donated 100 francs and soon heard the announcer saying that this time the prize had been given by 'Le BBC de Londres'. In order to explain instantly what we were doing and especially to make Jamie and Rupert's lives easier as they went ahead each day to find fields for the horses, I had prepared and photocopied a short description in French of our intentions, over a photograph of two Camargue horses (not in fact Thibert and Tiki, as I had not had time to have any prints of them made). On the back was the rather glowing blurb from the cover of my autobiography which had just been published in France. We hoped that, used rather like a circus flier announcing our imminent arrival, it would help to secure us a friendly reception wherever we went.

I now sent Rupert up to the announcer with one of these fliers and she duly told the assembled crowd something of our plans. It was hard to judge their reaction as many were well away both with the excitement of the event and the large quantities of wine they had been drinking since dawn, but it did at least explain what our film crew were doing there.

The whole contest seemed to us a most delightful and acceptable form of bullfighting. As each bull lost his trophies in straightforward contests between an unarmed man and a well horned animal, it was driven from the ring and would be later returned to its herd so as to take part in future contests. This is achieved by a single *gardian* driving each bull at breakneck speed through the crowded streets and out into the open country beyond. It is reminiscent of the bull running at Pamplona in Spain as young men show their courage by standing in the way until the last moment, and it is astonishing that people are only rarely hurt. At this time both the bull and horseman are united in knowing where they are going and wishing to arrive there as soon as possible. Great *cocarde* bulls are respected, venerated almost, in the Camargue; they perform for many years and after they retire and die of old age their names live on in legend. When an old bull dies it is said that the whole herd will gather round the body and bellow in unison. This is called making Ramadan.

Rupert is always firmly on the side of the animal in any contest and this, combined with the excitement and danger of it all, made him long to spend more time there, ideally to see a whole week's fête through. He and M. Fauvet had become particular friends, recognising each other across the generations as natural allies. That evening while we went to stay with Maggie Skeaping, Jamie and Rupert dined with the Fauvets and Rupert became less self-conscious about his French as they discussed the day's thrills. By bedtime it had been agreed that my son should return during the following summer holiday and stay with the Fauvets and take part in the fête on a borrowed pony. I was glad that he would still be too young to be a *razéteur*.

The next day was a Sunday and we gave the horses and ourselves a rest. It was a chance to repack the car together with Jamie and Rupert so that they should, in theory at least, know exactly where everything was and have no excuse for not keeping it tidy. We also reconnoitred the route for the next day's ride. It involved crossing several main roads, a motorway and miles of built-up suburbs of Montpellier in order to avoid the centre of one of the few major cities which lay directly on the route, and I was worried. Whatever route we chose looked like being

STATION
BODMIN PARKWAY

**MAIDENWELL
CARDINHAM
BODMIN
CORNWALL**

PL30 4DW

TELEPHONE
CARDINHAM (020882) 224

Explorateur britannique et sa femme
font une randonnée équestre de Camargue en Bretagne

-.-.-.-.-.-

Robin et Louella Hanbury-Tenison vous prient de bien vouloir
leur aider quand ils passent chez vous

"Aux mois d'Août et Septembre ma femme et moi avons l'intention d'aller de
Camargue en Bretagne à cheval. Nous prendrons ensuite le ferry à Roscoff
et nous continuerons à cheval jusqu'à notre ferme en Cornouailles. Nous
avons acheté deux chevaux hongres Camarguais.

On m'a demandé d'écrire un livre sur ce voyage et j'espère qu'il
encouragera d'autres personnes à profiter des merveilleuses possibilités
que la France offre aux amateurs de randonnées équestres. Notre expédition
sera également le sujet d'un reportage pour la télévision, RTF3 en France
et BBC en Angleterre.

Je joins à la présente une photocopie de la couverture de mon
autobiographie qui vient d'être publiée à Paris et qui vous en dira un
peu plus sur moi."

Robin Hanbury-Tenison

Extrait du couvert de l'autobiographie de ROBIN HANBURY-TENISON

DES MONDES A PART
(publiee par Robert Laffont, Paris Avril 1984)

Un itinéraire vraiment unique. Sorti d'Oxford pour se lancer dans l'aventure ou, comme il le dit, « l'exploration pour l'exploration », Robin Hanbury-Tenison a parcouru le monde et accompli des « premières », des déserts africains aux sommets sud-américains, de l'aéroglisseur sur l'Amazone au plus grand gouffre du monde en Asie. Ses exploits lui ont valu d'être désigné par le prestigieux Sunday Time Magazine comme le plus grand explorateur des vingt dernières années dans une liste des autres « plus grands » où se côtoyaient de Gaulle, Yves Saint-Laurent, Pelé, Noureïev... et la reine Elisabeth.

C'est à la faveur de ces voyages qu'il a découvert qu'on s'occupait beaucoup plus de la protection d'espèces animales menacées que de la défense des groupes ethniques écrasés par la civilisation industrielle. Ainsi est né à Londres en 1969 **Survival International** qui, à l'instar d'**Amnesty International** — pour la libération des prisonniers politiques —, se consacre à la défense des minorités menacées d'extinction physique et culturelle — ce qui représente quelque deux cents millions d'êtres humains.

Chez les Indiens d'Amérique du Sud, en Indonésie, en Malaisie notamment, il a vu comment, au nom du progrès, les hommes disparaissent en même temps que les animaux et les arbres. C'est ce combat pour la survie de peuples et de cultures en voie de disparition et pourtant indispensables à l'équilibre du monde que raconte Robin Hanbury-Tenison dans ce livre, **Des mondes à part,** un combat parfois couronné de succès comme, par exemple, chez les Indiens yanomami du Brésil qui se sont vu accorder une « zone interdite » de près de huit millions d'hectares.

Président de **Survival International,** vice-président de la **Royal Geographical Society,** pour laquelle il a dirigé de grandes expéditions, cet Irlandais de quarante-sept ans, gentleman-farmer en Cornouailles, est, pour reprendre la formule du premier Français qui l'a découvert, Jean-François Fogel, « un grand voyageur devenu le commis des causes tribales ».

Robin et Louella Hanbury-Tenison

unpleasant and dangerous. M. Fauvet, when I consulted him, came up with the solution at once. He had a horsebox, didn't he? Our only disagreement was over whether I should be allowed to pay or not, an issue on which we both adopted immovable positions. In the end, both secretly resolving to win the dispute, we agreed to shelve the discussion.

Early on the Monday morning we reported to the Fauvet farm, loaded the horses and drove in convoy through the rush-hour traffic to the other side of Montpellier. Paul Nayrolle had given me a route from a village called Montarnaud and there we unloaded Thibert and Tiki and saddled them up on the steps of the church. John Perkins was there to record the moment and Maggie had come to see us off. As I kissed her goodbye and tried to thank her for being our inspiration and Guardian Angel throughout all the planning stages, I slipped her 500 francs to give to M. Fauvet as a contribution towards his petrol. Much later I heard from her that he had thanked me very much but said he would hold it as pocket money for Rupert when he arrived the next year. That round went to the French with honour.

We gave Jamie and Rupert their instructions for our afternoon rendezvous and clattered optimistically off up the steep cobbled lane.

Once we were out of sight the rest of our party made their *adieux* and prepared to go their separate ways. M. Fauvet climbed into his empty box and began to back it into the street. Rupert and Jamie in my fully loaded car did the same. There was a sound of grinding steel and breaking glass as, having approached from their respective blind sides, they met. But we were not to hear about that for some time to come.

4
The Magic Begins to Work

Aimé Felix Tschiffely, on his famous ride from Buenos Aires to Washington in the 1920s, took two horses which he describes as having originally been 'the wildest of the wild'. The first few horses were brought to the Argentine from Spain in 1535 and their descendants roamed wild for centuries. His two were formerly the property of a Patagonian Indian Chief called Liempichun, which he says means 'I have feathers', and they were already 15 and 16 years old by the time he acquired them. His book *Southern Cross to Pole Star* had always been a favourite of mine and I felt a special link with him as one of my own early expeditions had been the first river journey through the length of South America from the Caribbean to Buenos Aires. Now we were setting out to do something which, while much shorter and less arduous than his great adventure, would nonetheless give us a taste of what he must have experienced. It was also interesting to dip again into his book so as to work out the logistics of his journey and apply them to our own plans. Tschiffely took two and a half years to cover 10,000 miles, an average overall of about 10 miles a day. But he made many long stops and at the end says that he actually spent only 504 days travelling, which gives an average of about 20 miles a day. We needed to average about 25 miles on each riding day, I calculated, if we were to reach Roscoff in time to catch the ferry on which we had booked our passages.

Tschiffely makes two other observations in his book which struck me. Early on he writes,

in order to appreciate fully the friendship of a horse, a man has to live out in the open with him for some time, and as soon as the animal comes to a region that is strange to him he will never go away from his master but will look for his company and in case of danger seek his protection. By this time both my horses were so fond of me that I never had to tie them again, and even if I slept in some lonely hut I simply turned them loose at night, well knowing that they would never go more than a few yards away and that they would be waiting for me at the door in the early morning, when they always greeted me with a friendly nicker.

We looked forward to cementing the same sort of relationship with Thibert and Tiki, to whom we already felt much closer than any other horses we had either of us ever known.

Towards the end of his journey, after he had crossed into North America, Tschiffely says, 'Concrete roads are excellent for cars, but they are very tiring and hard on horses; and heavy motor traffic makes horseback riding anything but pleasant. Today, also, the problem of stabling horses in American towns is not as simple as it was once. Stables have given way to garages in most villages and towns, and sometimes even on farms.' If that was true nearly 50 years earlier, how much more might it present us with a problem as we crossed modern France. We resolved to try and keep off roads as far as we possibly could, even if it meant detours in order to stay in the countryside. At least we had Jamie and Rupert to seek out fields or see if stables still existed.

It was with high hopes therefore that we came across the first splash of red paint on a wall as we left Montarnaud and convinced ourselves that this was one of the signs which Paul Nayrolle had assured me marked his route. When it was succeeded by a clear red arrow painted on the ground to indicate where a stony track led off through a pine forest, we followed eagerly. Out in the farmland of the valley beyond, the paint marks were clear and frequent; only occasionally did we have to stop or backtrack to make sure we were still on the route. Once, when they stopped at an intersection, we separated so as to follow both possible alternatives and when Louella called out to say she had picked up the trail again, I cantered over the stony ground to join her. It was so good to be under way and following a cross-country route which led almost all the way to Rocamadour, where we planned to meet the BBC again in 10 days' time, that we blithely refused to be worried when, after a while, it seemed that we were going round in a circle. The reassuring reappearance of the paint marks at regular intervals lulled us into ignoring the warning signals sent out by our bumps of locality. Then, after an hour, a town which was unmistakably Montarnaud appeared dead ahead of us and with a dreadful sinking feeling we realised we were back where we had started.

Just then we saw some horses tied up outside a row of stables and a group of people sitting down to an early lunch at a table in the open nearby. We rode over and they said they knew nothing of any red signs but that the standard equestrian signal was an orange paint mark. As we rode on I had a tantrette, cursing myself for not having established that simple piece of information before. Louella resisted the temptation of saying that the directions we were taking had been worrying her for some time and rode in silence while I fumed. From then on I always kept my compass handy and we stopped constantly to check what we were doing against the series of IGN 1/100,000 maps which covered our route.

Abandoning our efforts to find Nayrolle's trail, we now followed the road for another hour until a point where, according to my marked map, the two should meet again. Here indeed was our first unmistakable orange sign leading us off into some wild country along a disused railway line covered in stony chippings. This in turn took us to the edge of a region of rocky hills and gorges through which a narrow well-marked trail led, giving us picturesque views and occasional glimpses of the road far below. Through scrubby woods of ilex, broom and a form of cactus we walked and cantered fast and happily, enjoying the certainty of being right all the more for the disastrous beginning. We even saw some piles of horse droppings, which were surely left by Paul Nayrolle's string of riders on their way down to the Camargue a couple of weeks before.

In Aniane we found our first proper horse trough. The horses were thirsty after their efforts in the heat of the day and it was a welcome sight as we clattered along the shady central boulevard. Cold, clear spring water gushed out of a brass tap into a stone tank. In spite of his thirst Thibert was suspicious. He snuffled at the surface, disturbing it with his nose as he shook his head up and down and it was some time before he would drink deeply. Tiki was, of course, much more sensible. We also drank and splashed our faces, while a courteous, elderly gentleman with a Panama hat and walking stick enquired where we came from and where we were going. For the first time, I replied airily that England was our destination and he was nice enough to express admiration for our courage and to wish us 'bonne route'.

It was not until we were approaching the Hérault river where it emerges from a deep gorge that John Perkins found us. He had been driving all over the countryside looking for us but was as cheerful as ever in spite of having spent a frustrating morning, and he told us that the boys had found a wonderful place to bathe and were happily immersed. Rounding a corner on the country road which we had now joined, we came on a sudden scene of intense tourist activity. Hordes of pink and brown bodies were stretched out on a wide gravelly beach beside the river far below. Tents dotted the few small fields; hot dog and chip stalls were doing a thriving trade; cars were parked everywhere along the road. The mouth of the Gorge de l'Hérault was spanned by a high spectacular 11th century bridge with a modern road bridge beside it. We stopped at one of the food stalls, bought some *frites* as we had had no lunch, and chatted happily to the proprietor and a group of French tourists who gathered round to pat and admire the horses. It was very hot and we were glad of a chance to buy cans of cold drinks. I offered some of my *frites* to Thibert who, I had discovered, was greedy enough to accept almost anything I gave him, but sufficiently well trained not to snatch at tasty tufts of grass or fruit as we rode past them. He quite liked chips, although the fact that they were still warm made him shake his head up and down and snort, apparently to cool them, which amused the bystanders.

As we nervously followed Louella and Tiki across the road bridge I kept imagining what it would feel like to find myself sailing down through the hundreds of feet of space below us if one of the cars passing tooted its horn at the wrong moment and Thibert shied violently sideways. After that, we were on the narrow track running between the road and the parapet over the deep ravine, from whence we had a far better view of the sensational scenery than had the people speeding past in cars. Even better, we could gaze uninterrupted as the river unfolded its extraordinarily romantic panorama beneath, leaving the horses to make their steady way up the steep and winding highway. Not for the last time we felt superior to all those who seemed to be missing so much of what they had come to see. It was a worthy beauty spot. The river runs at the bottom of a limestone canyon where the rock has been worn into weird and wonderful shapes. Sometimes there are shelves where the river used to run, from which cascades of light green ferns reach down to the lower levels where the water now tunnels under an overhang. Elsewhere there are fine waterfalls and below them deep, clear pools of a striking blue, in which huge trout can be seen basking in the depths. Turquoise kingfishers add an occasional touch of almost psychedelic colour to the already dreamlike setting.

Far up the valley is the extremely picturesque village of St Guilhem-le-Désert. It, too, has become a popular tourist spot, so that the narrow cobbled streets up which we rode were bordered by craft shops. But the French seem better than the British at coping with the problems posed by hordes of outsiders descending on an ancient and unspoilt community. Here, for instance, as in many other places, cars (but not horses) were banned from all the smaller streets.

We were to see many examples across France of places which had been discovered by coach tour operators and were subjected to annual invasions during the summer holidays without apparently losing their charm or being subjected to the worst excesses of trinket mania and cheap commercialisation which may be fun at some seaside resorts but strike such a jarring note when found in places where the very attraction drawing the crowd is the perfection of the architecture and the natural beauty of the setting.

In St Guilhem-le-Désert the little ancient houses were immaculately kept and lived in by residents who leaned out of their windows to watch us pass – and then re-pass, as John asked us to do it again so he could get more shots from a different viewpoint. On either side of the alley ran streams of clear water, once presumably the open drains, now uncontaminated probably as a result of the new found prosperity bringing a municipal sewage system and road cleaners. Many houses had window boxes with fine displays of flowers; one old lady in particular had an amazing display of geraniums all along the staircase leading up to her cottage. As we paused to pose against this fine backcloth, both the horses embarrassed us by depositing neat piles of manure in the street. I apologised profusely for their bad manners, but instead of screaming abuse at us, the lady was delighted and, grinning hugely, she hurried out with a shovel to gather up this rich and valuable commodity.

The Abbey church, which was consecrated in 1076, looked Byzantine to me, with its rounded apse of soft reddish stone and pantile roof. The cloister, I learned to my surprise, I knew already, as it had been removed to the Cloister Museum in New York, which I had visited with Marika to see the famous unicorn tapestries there.*

In the square an ancient spreading tree shades the fountain, where the locals were drawing water from the four gushing pipes. Here we dismounted and let our tired horses drink their fill once more.

Jamie had done well on his first serious test. Tracking down a lady who served on the town council of St Guilhem-le-Désert, he had persuaded her that we should be allowed to camp above the town in a municipal meadow, a place where, following the wise policy of encouraging tourism but preventing it swamping local life, camping was normally strictly forbidden. He told us all this with justifiable pride and was duly congratulated. Then, shamefaced, he confessed to having 'scrunched' my car, something he had managed to keep from me until that moment as only the wing was damaged and he had parked it facing away. To my own surprise my reaction was one almost of relief that he had got something pretty inevitable out of the way early on in the journey.

The setting of our camp was one of the most dramatic imaginable. The head of the valley is a stupendous natural amphitheatre. Sheer cliffs towered above us on all sides to form the Cirque de l'Infernet and behind us to the west the sun was already dipping towards the higher peaks. The horses were pleased to be unsaddled, rolled together at once, as they always did at the end of the day, and began contentedly to graze the coarse grass under the cliff against which our meadow lay.

* My late wife's obsession with unicorns dated from the research she did for the first book she wrote, which was published many years later, after she had become a successful cookery writer. It was a children's book called *The Princess and the Unicorn* (Granada, 1981) and resulted in her collecting examples of what she called unicorniana so that Maidenwell, our house in Cornwall, became crowded with examples of every sort, from inn signs to glass paperweights. We also searched out representations of unicorns wherever we travelled, finding them in the most surprising places.

We left them and drove back down the hill to sample the boys' bathing place. It was indeed wonderful, away from the crowds at a point where it was possible to scramble over the rocks and dive 20 feet down into one of the deepest pools. The water was prodigiously refreshing and swimming was the best possible therapy for relaxing our stiff muscles, so that we went on back to Aniane feeling terrific and ate a huge and delicious dinner at a small restaurant where the bill came to barely £4 a head including quantities of local wine.

Back in our meadow in the moonlight we found the horses lying down peacefully side by side. They were more prone to sleeping this way than other horses I have known and did not always bother to stand up when approached. We could go over to them and give them a goodnight hug without disturbing them. There was one scrubby thorn tree to which we tied our hammocks, the other ends being attached to the front and back of the car's roofrack. In this way we could lie side by side, within handholding distance, yet turn over in the night without disturbing each other. Jamie and Rupert slept in their sleeping bags on the ground in a sandy hollow next to the stream and John stretched out in his own hired car.

It was a glorious night, during which I was hardly conscious of sleeping at all and yet awoke feeling fully revitalised. Most of the time I lay gazing up at the great grey crags and castle walls looking over us all round and all perfectly visible in the light of the full moon. Opposite I could see the old gateway on the hillside through which we would leave in the morning and the faint mark of the track which climbed alarmingly steeply towards the ridge. Among the fine display of stars above, Louella spotted her first satellite, which we watched as it travelled from one horizon to the other. Each hour two sets of bells in the village tolled and I counted, since we had planned to make a very early start. But at five it was still dark, the moon having set and the sun not yet having any effect. Even at six when I began to wake the others it was barely grey, so deep in our valley were we. Only the ravens, flying high above the peaks and croaking noisily, seemed to be catching the first rays of sunlight on their wings.

The public lavatory in the car park at the top of the town provided both us and the horses with water, which we fetched in our bucket. It was built in a grotto right under the cemetery, the water apparently flowing from a natural spring below the graves.

We left on foot, leading the horses and travelling in single file up the narrow track. It was a serious climb, near the limit of what Tiki was capable of as he still wheezed, coughed and from time to time snorted quantities of phlegm. We worried at the wisdom of pushing him so hard, but there could be no turning back and so with frequent pauses we carried on. The scenery more than compensated for all our anxieties. To the south and east we could see forever across the plains. Only the tower blocks of Montpellier, 20 crow-flying miles away, broke the natural grandeur of the view. To the north-east stretched the tangled mountain ranges of the Cevennes, that wild desolate region through which Robert Louis Stevenson had walked more than a hundred years before, writing that childhood favourite and classic *Travels with a Donkey*. His companion Modestine, of whom he writes touchingly at times, clearly drove him wild most days, suffering all the 'faults of her race and sex'. We had hoped to retrace some of his route, but it lay too far off our course and would also have involved much more hard country for the horses. He, too, had enjoyed his nights under the stars, but as he describes towards the end of the book he was not as fortunate as I was.

> And yet even while I was exulting in my solitude I became aware of a strange lack. I wished a companion to lie near me in the starlight, silent and not moving, but ever within touch. For there is a fellowship more quiet even than solitude, and which, rightly understood, is solitude made perfect. And to live out of doors with the woman a man loves is of all lives the most complete and free.

Stephenson also gives a prophetic foretaste of his famous epigram 'to travel hopefully is a better thing than to arrive, and the true success is to labour.' In this book, when travelling through a particularly harsh and barren part of the Cevennes, he writes,

> For my part, I travel not to go anywhere, but to go. I travel for travel's sake.* The great affair is to move; to feel the needs and hitches of our life more nearly; to come down off this feather-bed of civilisation, and find the globe granite underfoot and strewn with cutting flints. Alas, as we get up in life, and are more preoccupied with our affairs, even a holiday is a thing that must be worked for. To hold a pack upon a pack-saddle against a gale out of the freezing north is no high industry, but it is one that serves to occupy and compose the mind. And when the present is so exacting, who can annoy himself about the future?

This elegant summary of the escapist impulses which drive true travellers strikes me as being just as valid today as when it was written in 1879.

Our climb now became like a pilgrimage as we toiled on in a kind of worried ecstasy. Everything around us was so perfectly wild and beautiful, yet our concern to achieve the right balance between sparing the horses, while revelling in the magic of the moment, and hurrying along with eyes cast down so as to maintain the necessary speed to realise our

---

* In his journal, but omitted from the book, the following sentence appears at this point. 'And to write about it afterwards, if only the public will be so condescending as to read.'

rendezvous kept us tensely aware all the time. Much of France consists of patches of wild country among the fertile farmlands. It is as though Scotland and Wales were chopped up and scattered over England to make one patchwork whole, rather than the stark contrast between the Celtic highlands and the Anglo-Saxon lowlands. But sometimes even that wildness takes on another dimension, as though some areas of beauty have always moved people to recognise a special quality in them. So it was with the path above St Guilhem-le-Désert. The stony track wound between contorted pine trees, around great boulders which seemed to have dropped from the sky, past stunted ilex and juniper, wild lavender alive with bees and covered in blue, red and yellow butterflies. It looked and felt as though it had been well trodden over the centuries and, sure enough, near the summit of the range we came on a secluded chapel, a place of great peace and sanctity, I felt, tucked into a dell and surrounded by taller, tended firs: the Hermitage of Notre Dame de Belle Grace.

Beyond the high hills we entered a less severe but still wild region which reminded me of the African veldt. Open grassland, though with more thistles, weeds and thorny scrub than grass, was intersected by belts of scrub oak forest, where we rode through open glades feeling like an Arthurian knight and his lady. Nothing would have surprised us, the enchantment of the day was so strong. Even when we arrived in a large and apparently abandoned farm complex, a fortress to which no hard road led, we were more taken with the beauty of the place than concerned that it proved we must have lost our way. When two elegant, bohemian ladies in hippy dresses, with beads and a baby appeared from one of the buildings and kindly gave us directions, we chuckled together for a mile or more as we cantered away because that time we had resisted the urge to explain ourselves. For once it was fun simply to have appeared and vanished like appropriate apparitions. We knew that we were cantering across France and that that was absolutely the best thing in the world to be doing.

When we emerged from a stretch of forest to see before us a perfect walled and turreted medieval town set in an empty landscape like the vast backcloth to a Renaissance painting, the pleasure was almost tangible, especially as that was where we had arranged to meet the boys. With time in hand we let the horses amble down towards the valley. Entering more forest we came upon lush green grass in patches under the trees and dismounted so as to let the horses loose to graze. We stretched out relaxed and happy, relishing the prospect of the carefree days which stretched ahead when there should be many such moments.

I dozed off to be awoken by ethereal music. Opening my eyes to see the evening sunlight slanting through the leaves and stippling the bank on which we lay, it was easy to imagine that I was dreaming. The music came closer and we sat up together looking at each other in smiling amazement. Then over the rise appeared a flock of sheep with bells around their necks; unattended and totally ignoring us and the horses, they strolled past and the music faded into the trees with them.

5

La Vie à Cheval

Often we stayed in inns instead of camping out. Once off the tourist routes, hotels were so cheap as well as being clean and comfortable that with the extra driving often involved in camping, as well as the washing of clothes and bedding, it was easy to persuade ourselves that we were actually saving money. When a double room with private bath or shower cost 60 francs or less, or about £2.50 a head, little more than the price of a gallon of petrol, we tended to spoil ourselves. Also, during the first weeks we did feel a bit stiff after up to 10 hours in the saddle, so that a good soaking in hot water was, we felt, medically wise. However, thanks to our leather chaps, we neither of us suffered a single blister, or were rubbed sore, throughout the ride.

The first hotel we stayed at was in a small town called Le Caylar (almost the same name as the village where the *abrivado* went). The boys, as usual, were sleeping out, this time beside the swimming pool of the kind family who had let us leave the horses overnight in their paddock. We only put *them* in a hotel for the night when we felt it was time for them to have a bath, or when it rained. After all, we argued fairly convincingly, it was more fun at their ages to camp and, besides, they could keep an eye on the horses if they slept near them. Best of all, they could have them ready for us by the time we arrived at dawn. We sat up late studying our maps and writing up our journals. This time the bathroom was along the passage and by the time Louella was ready for a bath it was 10.45 p.m. When I took her place some time later and ran more hot water, the pipes juddered and groaned. The next thing I knew a furious harridan was beating on the door screaming imprecations about it being an unholy hour to take a bath. I had not bothered to lock it after Louella's departure and to my horror it burst open so that I had to leap out and push it shut in her face. I waited until things quietened down before scuttling back to our room clutching the minuscule towel, which was all I had with me, around my waist. French hotels are seldom generous with their towels. Fortunately we had paid that evening and so were able to tiptoe out at six before anyone else was awake.

There was no fixed pattern to what we did for lunch. Sometimes we met the boys for a picnic at a spot preselected from our maps the night before. There was always a supply of pâté, cheese, sausage and wine in one of the tin trunks on the car roof and Jamie became expert at finding fresh bread, fruit and delicious pastries. At other times we would rest the horses for an hour on a village green taking turns at watching them and eating a snack at a café. Often we simply left it to chance, planning the evening rendezvous, letting the boys go off for the day to explore once they had found a field for the horses that night, while we waited to see what we found along the way. If we found nothing our appetites were all the better in the evening when we always ate out – and never once badly.

If I found it surprising that country inns could make a living from what they charged for a night's lodging, the economics of the *prix fixe* menus left me completely mystified. The cheapest menu was sometimes as little as 32 francs (under £3), seldom as much as 50 francs (just over £4) and for that we would be served four, five or six courses and often wine as well. Not only was the cheapness an attraction; these menus provided the perfect way of sampling the local products as we passed between regions without having to do the research necessary to find out what to ask for. Cheeses especially were very localised and our taste-buds were frequently expanded dramatically as we experimented with whatever was placed before us. The pâtés, rillettes, charcuteries, salads and local foods also provided a seemingly endless variety of local specialities.

One of the happiest picnics was on John's last day with us, which was also his birthday. Perhaps because it was tinged with sadness at his departure, we were all in exceptionally good spirits. I had briefed Jamie to buy some special delicacies for the occasion and, when we all met in the central square at La Cavalerie, we found that John had brought some champagne. We tied our horses to the plane trees outside the Mairie, unsaddled, fed and watered them; then, sitting on the low wall by the fountain, we tucked into thick slices of Bayonne ham, spicy salami sausage, a rich goat's cheese – the chunks all held in long, crispy, fresh loaves of bread. The birthday cake was superb, mouthwatering strawberry cake. A friendly family, whose house overlooked the square and who had interrupted their own lunch to come out and admire the horses, presented us with a bottle of Alsace wine which went well with the cake. Behind us rose the ancient walls of the Commandery or manor of the Knights Templar, who were powerful here in the 12th to 14th centuries, with an especially pretty gateway into the old town beyond.

We climbed rather unsteadily back into our deep, safe saddles, John took some final photographs and drove off. He had been a perfect companion, undemanding yet highly professional when at work and always fun to be with. His photographs in the *Telegraph Sunday Magazine*, which came out that October, managed incomparably to capture the magic of what we were doing.

Beyond La Cavalerie stretched a wide, open, rocky plain, the Causse Noir, which reminded us strongly of an arid Bodmin moor. Rocky tors, dolomitic limestone instead of granite, but similar from a distance, rose from barren, stony ground across which we were able to travel fast, the wind in our faces helping to clear our heads. On the dry earth flourished attractive cornflower blue thistles and another variety which grew flat rather like a sunflower head sunk into the soil. We saw these sometimes nailed to the doors of houses as holly wreaths are at Christmas. Splashes of colour appeared when there were scarlet poppies. Birds were extraordinarily scarce, though we often saw empty cartridges which showed that someone had been shooting something. Apart from one huge covey of about 50 partridges, which we put up far from any road on the Causse Noir, only larks and ravens, both high in the sky above, were to be seen regularly.

It was thirsty country for horses, without streams or water troughs. Instead, near farms, we had during the preceding days often passed circular water-holding pits made of cobbles or brick, some of immense size but mostly nearly dry at this season. They appeared to be designed to catch flood water, there being sometimes a mud trap with a metal grille at the end from which the water could flow down into the pan. Many were beautifully constructed, but our horses did not like them. Even when led reluctantly down the sloping sides to the water at the bottom, they often refused to drink even when they had had none since early morning and we soon learnt the truth of the proverb, 'You can lead a horse to water . . .'

The plain marked the very edge of the Massif Central, across a corner of which we had ridden after climbing up from the delta of the Rhône, and which we would now be skirting for some time. At Millau, the escarpment drops almost sheer for 400 metres to the Tarn. We camped right at the edge in a grove of trees where once again there was lush grass for the horses to graze, though no fence to prevent them wandering in the night. Since there was a main road not far away, we thought it safest to tether them to trees. This they did not like, circling round their moorings, trampling the undergrowth and causing me to pass a restless night leaping in and out of my hammock to unwind them, a painful and dangerous operation in bare feet in the dark. The others all slept soundly, blissfully unaware.

Earlier that evening I had driven down the precipitous, hairpin road into Millau to make the first of my telephone calls to Woman's Hour, the BBC Radio 4 afternoon programme. Sue MacGregor, the presenter, a long-time friend who had been staying with us in Cornwall shortly before we left, had persuaded me that this would be a good way of keeping friends and family informed of our progress. She is such a superlative interviewer that it was always fun to talk with enthusiasm about what we had been doing and especially how the horses were bearing up. When, on this occasion I mentioned that Tiki had had strangles, several listeners wrote in expressing concern.

After leading the horses down through the pine woods clinging to the sheer hillside in the early morning, we rode across the busy road bridge into Millau and climbed up through the suburbs above the town into a dramatic change of landscape. From a horse, although only travelling at a mere four mph, even slight changes are much more noticeable than from a vehicle, but this was as though we had crossed a frontier. Fields of barley and wheat were separated by hedgerows and sunken lanes making the prospect much more familiar to a British eye. The harvest was in progress and several farms had big modern bales of straw on them, though many still made stooks of corn with a reaper and binder. Climbing all the time, we reached a great hog's back ridge which was covered in fir plantations through which the GR62, which we were now following, was clearly marked. Over the top we came out to another fine vista, this time of rolling downs, rather like Salisbury Plain, stretching away to the horizon. The illusion was further reinforced by fine stands of beech trees replacing the holm oak and Spanish chestnut of Provence. Through these we could ride in peace on the dry leafmould, bare of brambles or scrub.

While Jamie rode Thibert for the final hour, Rupert and I drove ahead to find a further field than the one the boys had already arranged. The horses had done well and we felt they could go a bit further than planned, particularly as we were beginning to slip behind schedule at this point. Just before Salles-Curan, a resort on an immense man-made lake in which Jamie and Rupert had been swimming and where we planned to stay the night, we saw a group of pleasant farm buildings close to the road. Driving into the yard we found the family stacking bales of hay in a barn and we seemed to step back in time. Wearing nondescript, somewhat ragged clothes which could have belonged to any era, were three toothless old hags, one with a good beard on her chin, who giggled and grinned at me as I approached.

A blank-eyed youth stared open-mouthed, straw hanging from his lower lip, while other half-seen figures peered down from the rick. In charge, and feared by all, was Le Patron, an alarming sight in a floppy hat, who treated me and my spoken French to a fine display of Gallic scorn and indifference as I began to explain our *raison d'être* and needs. They found it preposterous and it was tempting to flee, but a copy of our flier and the offer of a ride in my car eventually persuaded him that there might perhaps be a suitable field we could go and look at. First he bellowed at one of the old women in patois to fetch something I couldn't catch. When she returned with a champagne cork I was mystified. It proved to be for plugging the water trough in an excellent small and well fenced meadow, where the grass was knee deep. On the drive back he became positively jovial, demonstrating that the most formidable ogres usually turn out to have soft centres. When I offered to pay for the grazing he at first said it was not necessary, but I managed to persuade him to accept 30 francs, the sum I had instructed Jamie to offer as an incentive to reluctant farmers. It was the only time in the whole of France when we were allowed to pay. Either my powers of persuasion were greater than Jamie's, nearly all subsequent negotiations being undertaken by him, or the combination of his charm and Scottish ancestry conspired to bring about a generous and free outcome each time.

We, too, had time for a quick swim in the lake that evening and in the morning rode alongside it for a while in the stillness of a dawn mist which turned the scene into a Japanese print. Long-masted sailing boats and little dinghys pulled up on the beach were reflected in the glass-calm water which, as the skyline was invisible, seemed like the edge of the sea.

Once away from the holiday resorts like Salles-Curan with its excellent hotels and restaurants, the region of Aveyron through which we were passing seemed very poor. Many of the farms had handsome old farm buildings, some of them clearly the remains of former great houses, but the dwellings themselves, although the land was rich, were mostly run down and badly cared for. We were saddened to see how often the fine roofs, lovingly constructed in wavy designs and intricate patterns from scalloped slates, were falling into disrepair. Inside the farmhouses were frequently glimpsed scenes of squalor more in keeping with a South American slum than the heart of the fertile farmland of a Common Market member. Everywhere we went we found traces of previous cultivation in places now deserted. This made our ride even more enjoyable as we could pluck the fruit from abandoned gardens and orchards without any sense of guilt; raspberries grew wild in the hedge-rows, and the blackberry season was just beginning; plums, damsons and greengages, whose taste I had almost forgotten, were plentiful, growing in the most surprising places. Hardly a corner seemed to have escaped the benign attentions of man at some time, and the hedges, instead of having been grubbed out to make way for modern farming methods, remained to bear witness to the past.

As we rode along I mused on the relative merits of travel by car and by horse. In a car there is the freedom to cover long and possibly boring

stretches rapidly so that time may be spent visiting cathedrals and
exploring the old quarters of towns. Speculative side trips may be made
to castles glimpsed on distant hills. Everything possible that may be
needed during the day, from wet-weather gear to cameras, film and
books can be carried in the car without effort and plans can be changed
on a whim. Against this there is the smell and noise inevitably associated
with car travel. Most important of all there is the pity of being insulated
by glass and speed from the world outside. Being confined to metalled
roads creates a preoccupation with logistics, time and the need to find
a petrol station.

Riding a horse puts one in constant and intimate contact with the
countryside. The smells, sights and sounds of the country are all around.
From a saddle hedges can be seen over; the skyline and ground below
the horses hoofs become one. There are inconveniences, too. In hot
weather flies will swarm around both horse and rider, while horseflies
too are no respecters of persons. Midges and mosquitoes have easy
access in their season. The very speed which seems so pleasant when
all is pleasurable may become frustrating when hunger or the desire for
a bath and bed grow strong and the distance ahead must still take some
hours yet could be accomplished in minutes in a car. As I had already
found out, getting lost on a horse is even more maddening than in a car
as it takes so long to backtrack and get on the right route.

The best thing about riding, especially on two white horses, is that
once the ice is broken almost everyone is friendly and interested. With
our leather chaps, check shirts and black Camargue hats, we were hard
to ignore although there were occasions when exceptional individuals
did manage it. We needed to cash some travellers cheques and this was
one chore which could neither be delegated to Jamie nor done in the
evening at the sort of inns we frequented. It had to be done at a bank
during daytime opening hours and that meant riding up on our horses.
In Pont-de-Salars, a small but busy market town through the centre of
which our route took us, we rode the wrong way up the crowded main
street among the shoppers. Half-way up we stopped outside the Banque
Populaire, whose plate glass window faced on to the street. Behind it I
could see a single cashier dealing with a customer. Conscious that it
would be hard to look more like caricatures of hold-up artists I pressed
the buzzer to be let in, handing Thibert's reins to Louella who had also
dismounted. A small crowd had gathered to watch, perhaps hoping that
we really would pull out pistols and rob the bank. The cashier, who I
now saw had a short beard and wore spectacles, glanced up. I tipped
my hat to him and without a moment's hesitation he pressed the release
switch and let me in. Thinking he might be shortsighted and feeling that
he could not receive many customers like us I strode up to him and

presented our cheques. But he played it straight and deadpan through-out, never commenting as Louella and I changed places so as to sign our respective forms. We remounted and rode on up the street with our money safely tucked away but feeling somehow slightly cheated.

As our journey progressed we began to learn more about the peculiar attitude of the French to travellers, particularly towards eccentric ones like us. I don't think there is any society in the world where the art of putting down a stranger has been refined to a greater degree. They greet one with an abrupt, dismissive manner. If they are unable or unwilling to provide the service or merchandise being sought, they seem to take a delight in saying so. I have come to the conclusion that it is all a pose to conceal their innate shyness and insecurity. As soon as the ice was broken, we found that without exception they were on our side and became eager to help far more than natural courtesy and politeness would demand. Almost everyone we met went out of his or her way to solve our problems. But first we had to throw ourselves on their mercy with smiles and a helpless air. Once we learnt to demonstrate early on that we posed no threat we were welcomed everywhere with a generous hospitality which should be the envy of the world, but is not, sadly, one of the traits for which the French are usually best known.

Evocative sounds bring back those sunny days riding through Southern France more forcibly than notes in my journal. Cowbells were ubiquitous – once a whole orchestra as we cantered unwittingly past a herd of dairy cows and caused them to take flight; the clip-clop of our hoofs as we passed through sleepy hamlets. These are a much more familiar part of the French landscape than they are in England. Usually they consisted of one large farmhouse with a couple of attendant cottages on a remote country road where there was no traffic. Our GR routes regularly led us through such places and our passing felt like the major event of the day, waking the dogs and making the cocks crow. Around Pont-de-Salars the country became softer and more rounded. Red earth as in Devon, small fields on the sides of rolling coombs, green lanes shaded with oak and ash, ideal riding country and uncannily like home at times when the buzzards mewed overhead, jays called in the woods and we came on secluded farms tucked into deep valleys. The cattle were different, being mostly white and of a breed unknown to me; so too were the lop-eared sheep who sheltered from the heat of the sun facing inwards in a dense cluster around a single shady tree. And the gnarled peasant faces above squat Bruegelian bodies were unfamiliar, too. Round-faced old ladies with whiskers and weatherbeaten skin; old men with leathery, wrinkled features from which sprouted great warts. Ducks on every pond. Village ponds, weedy and frog-ridden.

There were fortified churches here, too, which we would have liked to stop and look at, but what with getting lost once or twice a day we always felt slightly under pressure to keep on the move, except when the horses were being rested at mid-day for an hour. Often all we wanted to do then was to stretch out and sleep while Tiki and Thibert grazed. We wondered why churches had to be fortified in the 14th century. The first one was at Inières in the middle of nowhere. The second at Ste Radegonde near Rodez. There 32 hostages were shot by the Germans in 1944, the day before Liberation.

We camped by a river on the outskirts of Rodez before what turned out to be one of the hardest days of all. It was becoming very cold at night so that we were chilled in our sleeping bags and quite glad to be under way with a chance of hot coffee and rolls en route. This time we failed to pass a café before finding the red and white GR signs and taking to the woods which bordered the river Aveyron thickly all along the next stretch. For about 50 kilometres the river twists and turns at the bottom of a steep sided valley. It looked easy on the map and we had made an optimistic rendezvous with Jamie and Rupert to meet us on a certain bridge with a picnic. Almost as soon as we left the road we were in trouble. The footpath we were following was not suitable for horses, being very narrow, only six inches wide at times, running along a very steep crumbling slope above the river and being interrupted by fallen trees and great boulders. Thibert and Tiki did not like it a bit, being unused to woods, let alone steep hillsides. They were brave and followed where we led them but even we had trouble not slipping down off the path and we were worried they would fall. As it became worse we considered turning back, but there was no obvious way round on the map and the prospect of retracing the ground we had covered already, which would now be even worse eroded by our traverse was unattractive. We kept hoping it would improve. We reached a place where a smooth slope of rock lying at an angle of 45 degrees barred our passage. There was a crack in which I could get a foothold but Thibert's *seden*, by which I was leading him, was barely long enough to reach the top. While I pulled and Louella urged from behind he placed his forelegs on the rock, heaved himself up . . . and slid back off again. At the second attempt he somehow scrambled to the top. Tiki tried valiantly to do the same, and required less urging as he was clearly anxious to rejoin his friend. The first time he nearly made it before sliding back. The second time he fell right over cutting his offside knee quite deeply so that the blood flowed. We had to forge a new route around the rock which led perilously close to the edge of a sheer precipice but which he managed safely. Now, in addition to his runny nose and cough, poor Tiki had a wound which might well go septic and make him lame so that he would have to be rested for a week or more. All we could do was bathe it every day and anoint it liberally with antiseptic cream. In fact it healed amazingly quickly (several people had told us that Camargue horses were remarkable in this respect) and he never appeared to favour it at all, even on that day.

Emerging from the wood on to a country road we met a man on a motor bike and asked his advice about the best way to proceed. He recommended a long detour by road which was probably bad advice, as the track once we rejoined it had improved greatly. Time and again well-meaning people of whom we asked the way thought of what would be the quickest and easiest route in a vehicle and failed to realise how much quicker for us and pleasanter for the horses it was to keep off hard roads and go across country. But we were shaken by our recent experience and so wasted an hour or more.

In spite of all our troubles and detours it was hard not to feel happy in the beautiful gorge of the Aveyron. The twists, turns and detours we made gave us lovely views of the river winding below us with romantic villages and isolated homesteads tucked in under the forested cliffs and steep slopes which made navigation so difficult. Once there was a castle high on a rock guarding the valley but the river was deep here and we could not cross to visit it. Later we forded the river where two meadows faced each other across a bend. The horses waded in fearlessly until the water lapped their girths but they never stumbled on the submerged, uneven rocks and we surged gratefully out on the far side. Sometimes there was a cart track along which we could canter and immediately our spirits soared.

Just when we were becoming exhausted, we came to a bridge at Les Planques with a pretty little hamlet on the far side. As we rode across we were delighted to see the first café-restaurant of the day, with a family sitting at one of the sun shaded tables outside. Greeting them heartily we dismounted, unsaddled and, with the permission of the *patron*, released the horses in the adjacent field, and slumped down at the next table ordering cold drinks and sandwiches of pâté and ham. They turned out to be from Didcot and, most flatteringly, knew something of us already. The parents were both teachers and they listened attentively as we regaled them with stories of our adventures. It was when I found myself feeling irritated when their two daughters were more interested in catching wasps under their tumblers than in hanging on our words that I realised how far our journey had begun already, to use Stephenson's expression, 'to occupy and compose the mind'. When we met local people, our efforts to charm them were usually justified by the need to persuade them to give us food or shelter, to act hospitably to strangers come among them. There was a danger that we could become so preoccupied with our story that we might fail to recognise that other travellers had their own fund of experiences too, and good manners demanded that we should sometimes listen.

Shortly after setting off again we had a much more salutary lesson that not everyone found our mode of travel romantic and endearing. The GR signs were clearly marked now and we were able to make better progress for a time. Then the footpath began to be very overgrown and difficult to pass so that we had to get off and lead the horses around fallen trees and up steep banks through thick thorn bushes. There were also for the first time wire fences across the path, which had to be undone and tied up again behind us. None of this would have posed any problem for the walker, but it did not look as if anyone had been through on a horse for a long time. When I had visited the head office of ANTE, L'Association Nationale pour le Tourisme Equestre, la Randonnée et l'Equitation de Loisirs in Paris I had specifically asked if it were permissible to ride on footpaths in France and I had been assured that, with the obvious exception of paths that went over steep routes through mountains, we would be able to go anywhere marked with the red and white waymarks. As we struggled to clear obstructions out of the way, we felt the afternoon slipping away from us. It was very hot, we were all tired and sweating and Tiki's wound needed bathing and dressing.

Crossing one of the many narrow roads which wound down to the river, we saw a clear waymark on a tree beside a path which led off into the wood beyond. A rough gate, around which a walker but not a horse could squeeze, barred the route. I dismounted and began to move it to one side. Below us, in a steep little field, was a burly man stripped to the waist using a scythe to clear some bracken. He hurried over to us and asked aggressively if we had authority to use the path. I replied that we did not need authority as it was a Sentier de Grande Randonnée. 'Only for pedestrians, not equestrians,' he shouted. 'I have granted permission on that basis only.' Instead of producing a flier telling him how far we had come and where we were going, I was stung to reply with icy politeness that I quite understood and that it would be just as pleasant to go round by road. This was a mistake, as with hindsight I was quite sure that I could have talked him round and the detour by road added at least an hour of steep and hard going to our day. In fact this was the only time on the whole journey when anyone questioned our right to pass, although we did occasionally meet new wire fences across old trails and once or twice these were difficult to shift and replace.

Our tiredness was lifted by the sight of Belcastel in the evening sunlight – a beautiful and recently restored medieval castle well placed beside the river, with water meadows and a tiny village below it. Only a few more kilometres along the river brought us to our meeting point with the boys on the Pont Neuf. They had had a good day, washing clothes in the river, drying them on the stone parapet of the bridge and bathing below the weir. Having expected that we would arrive earlier and want to go further, they had not arranged a field, but two enchanting small boys of five and six years old took us in charge. They were called Stephan and Christian and they gave the horses and us the most fervent welcome imaginable, begging to be allowed to ride on the front of our saddles and goggle-eyed with admiration for our *courage*. Unhesitatingly they led us to the cottage of the owner of some land, secured permission for us all to spend the night there and showed us where it was. It proved to be a pocket-handkerchief-sized plot of grass on the edge of a small stream, hedged in only by some undergrowth and tall weeds. But we thought the horses would be unlikely to wander, especially if we slept next to them. There were trees to which we could attach our hammocks, and so in front of our fascinated and devoted audience we made camp.

There was then the question of dinner, since we had no inclination to leave the horses and drive miles in search of a restaurant. Stephan and Christian's parents ran the local café, a simple slate-roofed building, with a balcony overhanging the river. Madame said that she did not normally serve meals but she would ask her husband if it would be all right. He agreed to her rustling up something for us while we fed, watered, groomed and anointed the horses and then had a refreshing bathe in the pool by the weir.

We returned to the café expecting a simple supper and instead found ourselves tucking into what I still remember as the most perfect of all the delicious meals we had in France. Not because of the richness of the ingredients or their preparation; certainly not because of the grandeur of our surroundings, which were as simple as can be imagined – a bare wooden table next to the family kitchen – but because almost every ingredient was made by our hostess herself from materials she or her husband had either grown or caught themselves.

We started with rillettes of pork, succulent in home-made jelly, pressed in an earthenware terrine. This was followed by a light, small pasta cooked in a delicate garlic sauce. Then came a fresh trout each, caught that day in the river, Madame assured us. Next a big bowl of spicy garden salads tossed together with a vinaigrette was served at the same time as an extremely powerful local goat's cheese which gave us all amazing dreams that night. A bland fruit cake to calm the palate and hot chocolate followed by a walk in the moonlight down to our camp left us feeling wonderfully ready to sink into our hammocks. Of course we had also drunk throughout the meal an unmeasured quantity of the rough red local wine; the jug was simply topped up every time the level dropped. The horses were faint grey shapes in the night mist at the water's edge and the murmur of the stream lulled us to sleep.

6

'Vos chevaux vous attendent, Monsieur'

One more long day brought us to friends of friends who were expecting us at Villeneuve d'Aveyron. We planned to spend a couple of nights with them and give the horses their first rest for more than a week. All we knew about our host was that he had a *Montgolfier*, the delightful French name for a hot-air balloon. We arrived to find that the family were gathered to celebrate the grandmother's 85th birthday. Forty-three descendants had assembled, the wine and food were flowing liberally and we were instantly made to feel that we, too, were members of the clan. Plied with drinks, questions and friendship we were able to relax in the delicious knowledge that for once we would not have to be up at dawn and off again the next day.

That night there was a fireworks party. Jamie and I held the horses as rockets exploded overhead, some even crashing in a shower of sparks quite close to us. Thibert was alarmed and could, I think, have panicked if we had not been there. Tiki, as usual, took it all in his stride. He was, besides, very tired so that he looked thin and miserable when unsaddled and we worried about him. When ridden he was gallant and, apart from wheezing on steep hills and showing a tendency to drop behind when walking fast, more as a result of his youth and small size than through illness, we felt, he was always the braver and faster of the two when danger threatened or high speed was called for. But in the field we could see that his ribs showed, his back was not broad and solid like Thibert's but sloped away from his spine and he was beginning to develop a saddle sore.

From now on the treatment and protection of this was to be another of our daily concerns. While it never seemed to bother or hurt him, it troubled us and we tried a variety of methods to cure it and other small sores and wounds which both horses acquired en route. Both animals responded well to treatment but their reaction to the treatment itself was dramatically different. While Tiki stood patiently whatever was done to him, Thibert was suspicious of ointments and powders, while aerosol sprays were anathema to him. The very sound of a hiss was enough to make him jump and I came to use this phobia to make him pass obstacles he suspected of being lions by holding a hand over his tail and hissing, when he would invariably leap forward.

Even Tiki was surprised when our host decided to inflate his hot-air balloon at midnight. Illuminated by brilliant flares, its vast and colourful bulk began to take shape behind the house, accompanied by a roaring whistle from the burner, which convinced Thibert that the end of the world had come; and it was easy to believe that something uncanny was happening as the balloon filled to tower over the two-storey pantiled house. Perhaps fortunately, it proved too windy to attempt a night ascent and so it was deflated and packed away again.

A single day of rest is always a busy time, being an opportunity to catch up with all the things for which there are no odd moments or energy normally. Letter writing, telephone calls, washing, shopping were Louella's chores, while I drove 100 miles north to visit a *Maître-randonneur* who could advise me about country routes and footpaths across the next bit of France. We were soon to cross the frontier between two of the historic provinces of France, leaving Languedoc and entering Limousin. The going should become easier in time as we approached the richer farmlands to the north, but if we were to keep off roads, local knowledge would be just as necessary to spare us the problems of becoming lost and having to backtrack, with which we were already all too familiar.

I found a tough character, who reminded me forcibly of Harvey Smith, drilling a group of mostly rather stout teenage girls who were cantering their large and highly polished horses around an indoor exercise ring. From the adoring looks they cast in his direction as he cursed and swore at them it was clear that he was worshipped as a brutal taskmaster and a hero for his renowned horsemanship. The size and smartness of the shiny chestnuts and bays with plaited manes, bandaged tails and gleaming tack made Thibert and Tiki seem like scruffy ponies, beneath contempt in such a superior horsey establishment, and I expected to be put down. Instead I was welcomed with unqualified generosity, as he produced all his own laboriously annotated large-scale maps and handed them to me, only asking that I post them back to him once beyond their useful range. Since they covered much of the ground almost as far north as the Loire, this was more than I could have possibly hoped for.

Roger Mallet, one of the elite band of some two dozen *Maîtres-randonneurs* in France, had himself ridden several thousand kilometres on long cross-country expeditions. He said that we could all stay at his place and the horses could have a field when we arrived in a week or so. We were also invited to dine there then with himself and the students

ABOVE Thibert drinking,
showing John Skeaping's
saddle.

RIGHT Louella with the silver-
studded Portuguese bull-
fighting saddle.

ABOVE Asking a French peasant woman the way.

LEFT A stony track typical of the footpaths (Grandes Randonnées) which we were able to follow for much of the route.

RIGHT Bebastel overlooking the Dordogne river at La Cave, the scene of our almost fatal early-morning swim.

ABOVE Rupert being walked over by a vulture at Rocamadour.

LEFT With Fabian Kendall at the Rock of Eagles.

BELOW Discovering prehistoric cave paintings (20,000 years old) with Jean Magert, owner of the caves at Cougnac.

ABOVE Julie leading the cosmopolitan group of riders from Souzet to La Dormac.

RIGHT The impressive château of Jumilhac-le-Grand with its fantastically embellished roofs.

OPPOSITE The moated castle
of Montbrun unsuccessfully
besieged by Richard Coeur de
Lion in 1199.

ABOVE AND RIGHT Some vil-
lages still have water troughs
or fountains while at others
our horses were able to drink
from the communal washing
tanks.

LEFT An early start meant a stop for coffee and croissants later.

BELOW French farming is much more mixed than in England. Rabbits and ducks are found at about every farm, however big or small.

so that we could tell them about our travels. I returned feeling hugely relieved about the immediate future.

I was back in time to dine under the stars with our kind and hospitable host, now firm friends for life, who expressed convincing regret when we said that we really must leave very early next day if we were to stick to our schedule. The boys had had a happy day playing games and swimming with the innumerable children and grandchildren of the assembled families, but they had also dutifully cleaned all our tack as well as unpacking, tidying and rearranging all our varied camping and riding equipment. Louella was proud that, wearing Rupert's trainers and playing with a borrowed child's racket, she had managed to beat our flamboyant and energetic host at tennis in a needle match watched by a cheering crowd of his relations. The horses had had a day of complete peace grazing with enthusiasm when not stretched out asleep or being made a fuss of by a couple of the younger and horse-mad female members of the clan. It had been a good day for all of us.

Our host's family had once all been farmers around Villeneuve, but their land was now mostly abandoned. A little grazing was let here and there but much of it was returning to thickets made up of juniper, box and scrub oak. Only some of the orchards and vines were still being harvested. This was a common story in the region as we were to see during the next day's ride. Between Villeneuve and the Lot we passed several deserted farms, the old granges crumbling into ruins, the fruit trees neglected. It was excellent country for riding through, wild and open with uncultivated fields to canter across and fruit at regular intervals. But it was sad to see that for all the aid available from Common Market agricultural grants it was not worthwhile any longer to farm on the high ground, the *causses*. There is something wrong with a world where in many parts of the tropics over-grazing is causing deforestation, drought and famine, while elsewhere, in the temperate regions, it has become uneconomic to farm land which has been producing adequately for thousands of years. Life was hard for the peasants who tilled the poorer land and undoubtedly it is better for them now. Fifty years ago 50 per cent of Frenchmen worked on the land; less than 8 per cent do so today. The figures are even more dramatic for Britain where only 4 per cent of us are still farming. Yet ultimately it is food that keeps us alive. Although there are surpluses now, with three-quarters of the world starving the day may not be too far off when we will have to buy peace on earth by feeding the hungry. Perhaps we will see a return to the land then. There is an irony in the fact that the very prosperity of those in Europe who were once peasants contributes to the problems already faced by Third World farmers. The demand we create for cash crops like coffee, sugar, vegetable oil and peanuts causes governments to encourage their populations to abandon traditional agricultural practices in order to help pay off their country's international debts. As the best land is taken for this purpose, the remaining forests are cut down for fuel, timber for export and by farmers in search of land to farm. The result is all too often drought followed by famine. Another of the reasons for the number of empty farmhouses we saw is the Code Napoléon. Under this it is impossible to leave the family house to only one heir; it must be shared equally, which means that all the siblings must be bought off if only one is to live there. Often it is easier to let the house fall down than resolve the rows and litigation which result.

We dropped briefly down into the valley of the Lot to cross the river at Cajarc by a noisy iron bridge, which the horses did not like at all. After a snack on the village green we scrambled by a steep path up a dramatic cliff to another rocky *causse* of stone walls and scrub-infested fields which continued all the way to the next lush valley, that of the Célé, where we spent the night. This time we checked into the last available room at the small and friendly Hôtel des Touristes at Marcilhac while the boys slept in the horses' field, at the edge of the river. The great Benedictine abbey of Marcilhac, which once owned Rocamadour, is now in ruins, having been destroyed by marauding hordes of Englishmen during the Hundred Years War.

The field was in the middle of the village and beside it the water was deep and clear, held in a wide millpool while the main stream ran over a weir. Here we bathed at dusk, cooling off after the dusty day and unwinding from the tensions of finding somewhere for the night and sorting ourselves out. We splashed and fought and ducked each other, while the horses grazed the thick grass on the bank beside us, much too busy to pay any attention to our high spirits. As we swam in midstream we saw a flotilla of local ducks and ducklings paddling towards us against the current as they made their way home for the night. They looked like an Atlantic convoy, the young in single file, the adults forming a protective screen around them. Jamie and Rupert could not resist becoming U-boats, swimming under water to surface unexpectedly and cause enough confusion to make them hurry on without panicking altogether. They were brave and dignified, sticking to their guns with surprising determination and all made it safely past us to an accompaniment of outraged quacks.

Next morning we were rejoined by our friends from the BBC with a new French crew. They brought us mail and news from home. Howard Perks, the director, also brought the rain. After two months without a single drop falling, it had rained on his first day's filming in the Camargue. We had experienced nothing but scorching heat and clear blue skies since he had left. He had confessed to a secret fear that he might be a Jonah in this respect and, sure enough, it had started to drizzle during the night and begun to pour as we sat together having breakfast, seldom letting up during the four days he stayed with us. But it was good to see him again and fun to have someone intimately interested in our progress to whom we could tell our adventures and feelings two weeks after setting out.

The first shot was to be of us riding up the winding road which climbed above Marcilhac on to the edge of the huge plain of the Causse de Gramat. We took extra trouble with the morning's grooming, wore our best check shirts for continuity and looked nonchalant but interested as we rode into camera. We found a shamefaced group huddled under their umbrellas. There had been a misunderstanding and each had thought the other was bringing the film. Letters, contracts and telexes were produced and scrutinised to settle things and it was found that the French crew, a charming trio called Jean-Michel, Jean-Claude and Jean-Marc, were responsible. The film would have to be sent under police escort from Toulouse. This was bad luck for Howard, who had lost a morning's filming, but rather pleasant for us as we were able to ride on in peace and end the morning with a relaxed lunch with everyone else at a good restaurant in Espédaillac.

We feasted on *maigret de canard*, showed off our recently acquired knowledge of local delicacies such as *cèpes* and *morriles*, two of the local edible fungi which were just coming into season, drank too much strong Cahors *vin de table* and, when the film turned up with its escort, rolled into our saddles and continued north.

The horses' shoes were by now practically worn out. They had been shod just before we left but the constant hard work over stony ground and with inevitable stretches along roads had made them paper thin already. Paul Nayrolle had recommended a local blacksmith called Daniel and we had arranged to meet at the hamlet of Ladignac that afternoon. He was a strong, good-looking young man whose mobile forge upset Thibert when he turned on the electric bellows but who did a fine job and complimented us on the condition of our horses' feet after such a long, hard journey. Everything was filmed and Louella managed to arrange a couple of retakes of their parting kiss, but this did not stop him charging the fair price of nearly £5 per shoe. We would wear out two more sets before we reached home.

Now the moment had arrived for me to make my second Woman's Hour broadcast, this time from a call box in the countryside. While the French crew filmed and recorded our end and the BBC recorded in London, Sue MacGregor and I chatted happily about progress to date (on schedule), Tiki's health (worrying), the state of our backsides (excellent), food and drink (enviable) and what the locals thought of us (quite mad).

Every now and then we had to break off as I fed in more five-franc coins, it being impossible at that time either to receive incoming calls or to make reverse charge calls from public telephones in France. It was fun and a lovely way of being able to let our families know that all was well with us.

Jamie had found a good field nearby where we were going to camp and he and Rupert had gone ahead to put up the tent as it looked as though there would be more rain in the night. It was nearly dark by the time the filming was over and we had to hurry along a track through a forest to reach the field. An evening mist began to fall and an owl hooted as the horses, eager for their night's grazing, cantered on. They seemed more nervous than usual and in spite of the late hour Thibert shied at a white stone. 'Silly boy,' I muttered out of habit, 'it's not a lion.' Then, in the darkness of the wood at our side, I saw several large shapes moving between the trees. To my amazement I realised they were wolves. It was clearly impossible, but when I looked again there could be no mistake; a dozen large grey timber wolves were loping along a bare ten yards away from us.

'Louella,' I said, 'the wolves are running.' *The Box of Delights* by John Masefield was my absolute favourite book as a child. In it the evil forces always turn into wolves which can be half seen running through the trees. The heroes, Herne the Hunter and the boy Kay Harker, triumph riding on a white stag and a white pony. For a moment I was in the middle of a vivid childhood dream.

'Don't be silly,' said Louella, 'look at the height of that fence. It must be a zoo.'

It seemed a funny place to me to have a zoo, but after a while we came to a notice on the fence which proved her right; a new Safari Park was being created in the woods. Strangely, nearby Gramat has the French Police Training Centre for Handlers and Dogs. We wondered if a little original blood was mixed with the wolf-like police Alasatians to make them extra fierce.

We slept in the tent, with the boys outside while the rain held off. There was a faint moon as I made a last check on the horses before turning in. They stood motionless side by side, shadowy figures rising out of the mist. As one we turned our heads towards the sound when a single faint howl came from the woods beyond the field.

It was some years since I had slept on the ground, hammocks being much more comfortable whenever there are trees, and I had forgotten how hard it can be. As a result I was restless and thrashed about. Louella dreamt that Tiki had come into the tent, feeling lonely, and was kicking her. 'Get out, you silly horse!' she shouted. 'Go back,' giving me a resounding clout. Soon after it began to rain in earnest so that Rupert joined us, to snore and roll about in his turn, while Jamie chose to curl up in the back of the car. As a result, we were all fairly bleary-eyed in the morning.

One of my most evocative memories of our ride is of the way Thibert and Tiki always hurried over to us in the morning. It was really only because they were greedy and wanted their morning meal, but it made us all feel that they were fully members of the team when they appeared to be asking to be saddled up so that they could start each day's journey. Instead of having to be caught we only had to whistle and they would come to us. That day they were invisible; a wall of fog surrounded us and for a moment I wondered if the wolves had had them in the night. Then we heard pounding hoofs and they cantered together out of the mist shaking the water from their manes and looking beautiful. Urgently they nuzzled us as we fumbled to fill their buckets from our sack of corn. They poked their heads in everywhere to find out what was going on, looking inside the tent flap and through the car windows. Although he still had a runny nose and coughed a lot, Tiki seemed to have picked up since the BBC had rejoined us. He was unmistakably camera-conscious. Normally he would tend to slouch along, his head hanging and his ears back. The moment he heard the whirr of a television camera all this would change and he would prick his ears, arch his neck and appear to make a special effort to look pretty. He also has an extraordinary way of standing when resting which I have not seen another horse adopt. He crosses his back legs like a ballet dancer, which gives him a relaxed and rather effete air.

Thibert, by contrast, stood four square on his sturdy legs, deceptively concealing his nervous disposition behind a robust frame. He was the horse whom everyone admired as a fine specimen of his breed, little guessing that in his breast there beat the heart of a mouse or that he needed his brave little friend to lead him whenever he was frightened.

Double-wrapped in our waterproof capes with Barbours underneath against the driving rain, we rode towards Rocamadour. The view as one arrives at the edge of the gorge is one of the most spectacular in France. Coming from the south the whole village is presented on the opposite cliff face, the picturesque houses and castles apparently stuck on like swallows' nests as they defy gravity, suspended more than 1,000 ft above the Alzou river winding along the bottom of the valley. We were duly filmed riding down the tortuous road with the view behind us; and then again coming up the narrow cobbled streets lined with trinket shops and cluttered with tourist buses. A good place to see, but one where there is no temptation to linger as the centuries of exploitation have coated it with a veneer that makes even the genuinely old bits seem like Disneyland.

The year before, on our reconnaissance, Louella and I had stayed at a delightful inn six miles north of Rocamadour, the Hôtel Pont de l'Ouysse at Lacave, and this was where we had arranged to spend the next two days, resting the horses and doing some filming on location. A huge spreading chestnut shaded the terrace where tables and chairs were set out for dining superbly in fine weather. We rode up in rain to be greeted like old friends by M. and Mme Chambord, the working owners (he is a celebrated chef) and Raymond, their maître d'hôtel. Whether they genuinely remembered us or were simply being flattering to customers who had returned bringing a whole film crew, did not matter. We felt extremely glad to have arrived. They pointed out a large grassy field across the river and next to the main road. We would be able to watch the horses graze from our bedroom window, although taking them there involved crossing by the bridge, half a mile upstream.

Once we had changed into dry clothes and settled into our rooms, Jamie and Rupert too in view of the heavy rain, we all sat down to a hearty late lunch at a table for ten behind the French windows in the main dining room. Having missed out on breakfast and after a hard morning's work for all, our appetites matched the excellence of the food. We all tucked in, intent on forgetting the cares of the world for a while.

As the main course was being served, a hopelessly rich and irresistible *confit d'oie* stuffed with *foie gras* and truffles, Raymond came and coughed apologetically behind my chair. When I stopped eating, he said, '*Vos chevaux vous attendent, Monsieur Tenison.*' At first I thought I was wanted on the telephone by someone. Then, as we all looked up, we saw that Thibert and Tiki were standing outside the French windows in the rain under the horse chestnut tree among the tables and chairs, looking in at us. I still cannot fully understand how they did it, but they had escaped from their field, made their way along the dangerous main road and over the busy bridge, down the lane leading to the hotel in order to be near us. Their pleasure when we ran out to catch them was evident and they wickered appreciatively as we petted them and gave them lumps of coffee sugar. They must have been lonely.

7

Caves, Birds and Balloons

After passing Rocamadour, the Alzou joins the Ouisse which then runs into the Dordogne at Lacave. Here the great river turns to the north forming a fine limestone cliff to the south while leaving gravel banks opposite. Poised above the precipice is the picturesque château of Belcastel. Privately owned, and with a dazzling view out over the curling river, the setting is straight out of a fairytale when its turrets catch the first rays of the early morning sun. Across the valley is a farm where flocks of white geese graze the grass like sheep. After the pâté and succulent goose meat on which we had gorged ourselves the day before, we could hardly bear to look at them. I for one was unable to do justice for the rest of our stay to the rich Quercynois food served in our excellent hotel, which lay right underneath the château.

The Dordogne river used to be the artery of Aquitaine, the old English Duchy, whose name means Land of Waters. Boats used to trade right up to and beyond Lacave. Until the last century teams of up to a hundred men hauled barges upstream. The commodity they sought was the very stuff we had been pushing through on our horses as we rode across the *causses*, the juniper which still grows there wild and plentifully. There was a huge demand for juniper berries by the Dutch who imported tons from here for making into gin. The name itself is an abbreviation of geneva which in turn comes from the French *genièvre*, meaning juniper.

The horses were now to have two days of rest, but there was to be no such peace for us with the film crew there. Every minute was costing money and should be usefully filled, even if Howard's ability to attract rain was working overtime. By mid morning it was pouring down. Soaked from an abortive effort to do some filming back in Rocamadour, we gathered in a café, drowning our sorrows in hot coffee and the occasional *fine* (cognac). More material was now urgently needed since with the delays through having no film on the first day and the rain on the next, relatively little had been achieved. Something had to be done, but what? Howard caught my eye and with a purposeful air we got up and left.

In France the tourist offices are called by the impressive title Syndicates d'Initiative and there were two in Rocamadour. We felt that this was a time to see if the initiative existed. At the first one my stumbling explanation of our needs received a completely blank response. A sheaf of illustrated leaflets on the sights and entertainments, hotels and restaurants of the region were thrust at us and no further advice was given. Feeling foolish but also very desperate as time ticked away and the crew remained idle we went to the next. Here we were greeted by a round, smiling lady who exuded confidence. Encouraged by a prod from Howard, who spoke no French, I handed her one of our fliers and launched in again.

'You see, Madame,' I said, 'we have a complete television crew here making a documentary about riding two white horses across France. Today we want to do something on the region we are passing through, which will make the story interesting, but it is raining and the sequences we had planned on the eagle sanctuary and the local scenery are impossible. Can you suggest anything?'

'Of course,' she replied, 'I think I know just the thing. What this region is perhaps most famous for is the great number of beautiful caves in which prehistoric art has been discovered. Indeed some of the pictures are even of horses. Would you like me to arrange for you to visit and film in one of them?'

Suddenly it all fell into place. Prehistoric art has always been a special interest of mine. In the early 1960s I made several long journeys through barren mountains in the Southern Sahara in search of one of the world's greatest but then almost unknown collections of prehistoric pictures and engravings. Travelling by camel with a Tuareg guide I had explored the Tassili N'Ajjer attempting to find and film for the first time the numerous beautiful paintings which had recently been discovered there. Glorious multicoloured pictures of wild animals and domesticated cattle dating from between 1000 BC and perhaps 8000 BC, they proved that the region was once fertile and wet. Many have since been destroyed by subsequent visitors and groups of tourists washing them to heighten the colours and I was lucky to have seen them in their pristine state. I also wandered by camel through the Aïr Mountains in Niger looking for more sights and, with John Hemming, managed to visit the war torn Tibesti Mountains in Chad during one of the brief lulls in fighting when it has been possible to go there. I had always dreamed of seeing the great caves of France where the art is so similar, yet dates from 20,000 years earlier. Lascaux I knew had been closed to the public for some years to prevent the paintings being destroyed by the atmospheric changes introduced by visitors. I had not realised that there were so many more that were still open.

The nearest cave, our helpful lady told us, was at Cougnac just outside the town of Gourdon and only 40 km as the crow flies from Lascaux. She telephoned the Director at once. Incredibly, he agreed in principle that we could film there, but said that we must come and see him right away as he would shortly be going to lunch. Thanking our angel effusively we dash back to the others, leapt into our respective cars and drove hell for leather to catch him.

M. Mazet, who turned out to be the discoverer and owner of the cave as well as the Director, was just setting off as we arrived. Dressed in thick corduroy trousers and Wellington boots he had mounted his bicycle and was about to pedal home for lunch. Cheerfully agreeing to delay this most important meal 'but only for five minutes' he led us to the cave entrance and we all trooped in behind him. As he turned on the lights and we followed him at a trot through a succession of chambers we were greeted by one magical fairyland after another. I have never seen stalactites and stalagmites so well presented nor forming such an enchanted forest. And in the last chamber beautiful paintings of mouflon, goats, deer, humans and even elephants. But there was no time to stop and look. We were simply there to see if filming was feasible. Louella and I began to giggle as we realised how dreadfully we were all behaving. Confronted by a fabulous natural wonderland ending in a great gallery of fine prehistoric art, all we could do was talk of lighting and camera angles. When someone called out 'Never mind the stalactites, where are the power plugs?' we were afraid M. Mazet would take offence at our unmannerly attitude to his beautiful cave, but his good humour never deserted him and he readily agreed that we could come back that evening with our lighting equipment after the last tourists had gone and film a sequence then.

Jean Mazet is a remarkable man and his is a strange story. He was a local boy and he had always had an interest in caves. His job took him away, but he usually tried to get home for the weekends. One day in 1949 an amateur water diviner in Toulouse whom he had never met contacted him. He said that after studying a large-scale map of the Département of Lot, a region totally unknown to him, he had come to the conclusion that a 'vast cavern' existed on the edge of Gourdon. M. Mazet was fairly sceptical but he had a look around at once. Almost immediately, within a hundred yards of the spot the diviner had marked on the map he found the blocked-up entrance to a cave. With the help of some local farmers he began to dig out the chamber which was filled to the roof with earth. After several months' hard work they broke through into a spectacular cave where some of the larger stalactites met fat stalagmites to form great pillars as in a grand hall, while a shower of smaller ones fell like rain or chandeliers from the ceiling. It is still today called the Great Entrance Hall. Encouraged by the diviner and still following his instructions M. Mazet and his friends dug further into the hillside on Sundays and during their annual holidays. In 1952, some 250 metres from the first cave, they came on another cave which, in addition to an even better display of limestone formations, contained one of the more exciting collections of prehistoric art to be discovered in recent years.

Shrewdly M. Mazet had bought up all the land above and so owned the caves. They now provide his livelihood, being visited by a constant stream of tourists while he (and who better) lovingly protects, studies and shows them off. He was certainly the soul of generosity to us, staying far into the evening as we filmed an episode where Louella and I chatted in front of the paintings and I compared them with those I had seen in the Sahara. More recently I led a large scientific expedition to the heart of the island of Borneo where, among our other studies, we had investigated the limestone caves of one of the mountains near our Base Camp. This turned out to be the richest caving area anywhere and our team discovered the largest cave in the world there, the Sarawak Chamber. One of the strange but true stories I was able to tell M. Mazet as we chatted during the filming concerned the snakes which inhabited those caves in Borneo. Up to eight foot long they lurk on ledges at the side of narrow passages between the chambers, from which the bats and swiftlets which occupy the caves in their millions, have to fly to reach their roosts. Striking like lightning in the pitch dark miles inside the mountain, the snakes catch them as they fly past. Like dragons they seemed to be guarding the entrances to some of the caves, which had lain undiscovered for as much as five million years before our arrival.

During the afternoon the weather cleared up enough for us to visit the other place at Rocamadour which particularly interested us. On the edge of the cliff above the Alzou river, just beyond the ramparts of the castle, an eagle sanctuary has been created. Over 100 raptors are kept there ranging from South American monkey eagles, to African vultures and local hawks which have been shot and wounded by hunters. The intention is to breed and return endangered species to the wild, cure and release the injured birds and meanwhile educate the public as to the beauty and importance of all birds of prey. To pay for all this it is open to the public and several times a day there are breathtaking demonstrations during which many of the birds fly free. Wearing heavy leather gauntlets the staff launch golden eagles out into space. With the thermals rising from the valley floor 1000 metres below, they are able to soar dramatically up into the sky until they are no more than specks, but at a signal from their handler they come swooping in low over the heads of the crowd standing at the cliff edge to land gracefully on his outstretched arm. The vultures were less elegant. They too flew out over the valley, but back on land they hopped about squabbling and fighting for scraps among the tourists. One of the vultures walked over Rupert's legs as he sat watching and a charming little kestrel delighted him by coming in to land on his head; at least he looked pleased as it perched there until it sank its claws into his scalp, which made him wince.

A young Anglo-French scientist called Fabien Kendall is in charge of the breeding programme and he told us about it all while the film crew did their stuff. He pointed out a handsome red kite whose handler was throwing scraps of meat high in the sky for it to catch with ease each time as it flashed past. This, he told me, was because it normally fed on insects which it caught in mid air. It had been brought in badly shot up and had responded well to treatment and was almost ready to be released. Soon the fifty or sixty pairs of breeding kites which survive in France would be beginning their annual migration to Africa. Some would be sure to fly over Rocamadour and he was keeping a watch for them. At the right moment, just as a pair was passing far overhead, he would free the cured bird. Although it was only two or three years old and had probably never migrated before it would, with any luck, fly up and join them, thus being instantly and effectively released into the wild.

As we watched, he pointed out far up among the clouds above us a faint speck which we could only just make out. 'That,' he said, 'is a wild short-toed eagle. It's watching what's going on. Lots of wild raptors come to watch our daily displays. They take a deep interest in what we're doing.'

One of the captive eagles, coincidentally also called Raymond, had developed the habit of diving down into the town itself where it would steal meat from the butcher's shop. Fabien told us that this had proved quite a problem, which had endangered the good relations between town and bird sanctuary. 'But in the end we cured him,' he said. We failed to ask how, and afterwards Louella and I speculated about ways of teaching an eagle not to do something. Aversion therapy? Meat tainted with bitter aloes? Housewives armed with rolling pins? Perhaps one day he will write and tell us.

Earlier in the year two of their eagles had been taken to Brazil to take part in a film. Made by the British director John Boorman, it was to be called *The Emerald Forest* and apparently concerned the building of the huge Carajas dam on the Tocantins river. The eagles' role was a 'symbol of the liberty for which the Indians of Amazonia were struggling, and of ecological stability.' Since these are two of the subjects closest to my own heart, I said I hoped that Boorman had done a good job and looked forward to seeing the film when it came out.

While there were, I gathered, those in the ornithological world who had expressed reservations about the work being done at the eagle sanctuary, we were impressed. The birds looked healthy and the daily free flights which so many of them were able to take took away much of the distaste one always feels at the sight of captive birds of prey. They were beginning to have some success with breeding and the team of handlers were patently zealous in their work. Certainly they were doing a good job in showing a very large number of people what beautiful creatures their charges were and getting across the message that it was a crime to shoot them. In a country where everything that runs or flies, however beautiful and proud in flight, however small and melodious in song like thrush, blackbird and nightingale, is shot on sight during the season, this is a message that cannot be delivered either too strongly or often enough. We had seen and heard for ourselves the lack of bird life in the countryside. It is a shame that a nation so supremely civilised in most respects should show such barbarity in this one.

With our long session at the Cougnac cave that evening it was late before we returned to the hotel after what had proved to be a very full and satisfactory day's filming. There we found our good friends from Villeneuve who had brought another couple, also *Montgolfier* owners. If the weather was kind they hoped to fly both balloons in the early morning so that horses, balloons and the fairytale silhouette of Belcastel could be filmed in glorious combination. As a result we made a large and noisy party, to which Raymond the maître d'hôtel was still patiently attending long after all the other guests had gone to bed.

The best time for balloon flights is usually just at first light when the air is often still. I crept out of the hotel at six to see what the prospects were and they looked quite promising, although the day was overcast. The horses' new field, one from which they could not escape, was down the road and I walked there to start getting things ready. Tiki did not look well. He was standing with his head hanging, his stomach tucked up and his ribs showing. As I gave him and Thibert their morning feed he perked up, but it was worrying as we would have to leave again the following morning. At that moment the clouds opened and I was soaked to the skin. At breakfast I asked Raymond if he knew a good vet and, as though it was a question regularly asked by guests, he gravely replied that he did and if I wished he would arrange a visit.

Serious ballooning was out of the question but one of the balloons was inflated for a captive flight. While an interested crowd caused a traffic jam on the road, the balloon filled and was anchored to two vehicles by long ropes. Louella went in the basket with the pilot and, to the accompaniment of loud bursts from the burner they rose some 20 metres into the air. Meanwhile I rode as close as I could on a thoroughly suspicious and excited Thibert, while leading a dejected Tiki who for once did not respond to the presence of the film crew. I don't think any of us had much idea quite what the scene we were enacting was meant to represent. The ingredients for something magical to happen were all there; the castle, the balloon and the white horses. But the rain kept interrupting the proceedings, the sky was black, the light poor and somehow the magic never came. I suspect Howard only set it up so as not to hurt the feelings of our balloonist friends and in the event none of the material shot was used in the film.

Just as it was all over and we were about to let the horses go for the rest of the day, the vet arrived and Howard decided to film that instead. He was a most charming and sympathetic man, who examined Tiki carefully while I translated his comments for the benefit of the film. He confirmed that the horse was still suffering from the after-effects of the strangles he had contracted before our departure and that a secondary infection might develop if we were not careful. He recommended a fresh course of antibiotics and showed me a better way of giving the 15cc mixture of penicillin and an anti-irritant. It involved shoving the needle straight into Tiki's neck instead of sideways into the muscle as I had done previously. That way there was less likelihood of abcesses forming. I was filmed as I administered the first of Tiki's five daily doses. Fortunately it went in smoothly and he barely seemed to notice. The vet said that under the circumstances it would be all right for us to continue our journey the next day, but that we should spare Tiki from strenuous exercise as much as possible.

After lunch the film crew and the balloonists departed. Within minutes the sun came out properly for the first time for four days and it was a scorching afternoon. The boys went for a swim while we sorted out our baggage, saddlery and finances. That evening our hosts the Chambords invited us in to drink champagne with them, wishing us well on the rest of our journey and toasting our *courage*. Over dinner Jamie and I vied with each other in brave talk about how much we enjoyed the early dawn, 'the best part of the day' when no one else was awake.

As a result, neither wishing to be outdone, we found ourselves leaving the hotel again at six a.m. to jog side by side down to the Dordogne for an early morning swim. The river was in flood and looked horribly wide. Whirlpools and eddies formed near the bank and trees were being swept past on the racing current. A fisherman sat motionless on the edge of a deep bay, his rod stretched out over the water. He barely acknowledged our hearty greetings and I suggested hopefully to Jamie that perhaps we should not disturb the fish by swimming near him.

'There's a great wee spot a bit further down,' he replied eagerly and sure enough there was a sandy beach where we took off our running shoes and plunged in. It was surprisingly cool for late August, fresh water I supposed flooding down from the heavy rains which must have fallen far up in the Auvergne during the last four days. I did a quick circle and emerged ready to jog home again. 'Let's swim across,' said Jamie.

Getting across was quite easy. It was on the way back that I began to wonder if I was going to make it. The current carried me towards a half-submerged tree trunk under which the water flowed and swirled. I took in a great gulp of water and felt my strength ebbing. It seemed such a silly way to go that I made a despairing final effort and at last felt muddy ground below my feet. As I sat gasping on the bank, my heart pounding painfully, Jamie kindly said that he had felt a bit stretched himself, which made me feel better; but I secretly vowed that that was the last time I would try and prove that I could swim as well as someone thirty years my junior. We jogged back to the hotel and all day particularly revolting water tainted with garlic and goose fat kept repeating on me.

We had coffee and croissants while the boys tried to give the horses a good grooming after their rest, when they had of course rolled regularly and made themselves filthy. We treated their feet every day with special grease to stop their hoofs cracking and this worked well. Two or three times they picked up a stone which had to be prised out, otherwise neither of the horses was ever lame as a result of foot trouble. Leading them for the first stretch, we climbed a steady track under the château to come out again on the plateau before dropping down to cross the Dordogne by a narrow and noisy iron bridge beside the pretty 17th-century Château La Treyne. Skirting the village of Pinsac we climbed again up into pine-covered hills through which a good track led, along which we could canter. As usual Tiki would lead when cantering, being faster in spite of his ill health, while Thibert thundered along behind. As we rounded a corner Tiki suddenly stopped dead so that we crashed into him. Ahead were two very smartly turned-out gentlemen on a huge bay and a chestnut. They were the first horsemen we had met since leaving the Camargue and they made us feel inferior and scruffy on our little off-white ponies and in our comfortable but rather shabby leather chaps and check shirts. Their high boots gleamed, their breeches were immaculate and they wore proper hard hats. We decided afterwards that they were probably the local doctor and solicitor out for a Sunday morning ride together. At first they were, as expected, rather superior in their manner to the two scoundrels who had so rudely disturbed the peace of 'their' path, but once we told them where we had come from and where we were going, the magic worked as it always did and they were charming in their expressions of good will.

After the crowded, touristy town of Souillac, where we had to ride along the tree-lined main street, we headed out into the countryside again, where the hedgerows were full of sloes, the blackberries and plums were ripening well and the tobacco crop was being harvested, the leaves dried in long wooden barns. Meanwhile the boys went for a trip down the Dordogne in rented canoes and had a lot of fun on the fast-flowing flood, while managing not to fall in.

We lodged the horses at a pleasant riding stables deep in the woods at Souzet. The owner, Jean-Paul Vergnes, had built a comfortable house with swimming pool where he took in guests for riding holidays, but his accommodation was full and so when the boys arrived, full of stories about their daring on the river, we all drove to Sarlat-la-Canéda. This is a beautifully restored medieval town where we were able to wander the streets of the centre, where cars are banned. The mellow beige local stone has been well used since the 12th century to build fine houses decorated with carvings and roofed with stone tiles. We rented a grand but quite cheap apartment above a café in the Place de la Liberté, sampled a wide variety of the produce of the local vineyards at a free wine-tasting and tracked down an excellent little restaurant where we gorged ourselves on the delicious food of Périgord Noir, one of the most celebrated gastronomic regions of France.

A group ride was about to leave when we returned to Souzet next morning. As they were heading in the general direction we wanted to go, we were invited to join them. For once we were relieved of the worry of trying to find our route across country. Instead we did as we were told by the pretty English girl who was in charge and who led the way. Her name was Julie and she came from Nottingham. She told us that she had found the job through answering an advertisement in *Horse and Hound*. There had been 400 other applicants.

We were a mixed group. There were two Dutch ladies of uncertain age who said they always travelled together, a German with his sweet 13-year-old daughter who was clearly horse-mad and loving every minute of her stay, a young French couple who, we suspected, were on their honeymoon and a rather overweight American receptionist from New Jersey, whose life's ambition was being fulfilled by this holiday. She rode very slowly and always brought up the rear, but her enthusiasm for all things equestrian, in spite of the fact that she could barely ride, made everyone forgive her.

We went slowly along open rides through a great forest consisting mainly of tall, thin scrub oaks, through which rays of light dappled the ground. Open, unfenced fields appeared from time to time and one sunlit glade reminded Louella of the bamboo groves in Jamaica where we had ridden on our own honeymoon when we had stayed on my brother's plantation. Sometimes Julie made us all canter, but mostly we just ambled along secure in the knowledge that she knew where she was going and that we could relax. Tiki, though he stumbled a bit and looked weedy beside the large and heavy horses of the riding stable, was cheerful and lively, clearly enjoying the unaccustomed company. Thibert was full of beans and would keep shoving his nose into the backside of the mare in front, for which he was kicked several times.

At lunch-time we rode up to a delightful inn at a hamlet called La Dormac where an excellent five-course lunch had been arranged in advance. The cheerful landlady fussed over us and made an embarrassing scene if anyone left anything on the plate. I sat next to Julie and we talked about riding in France and the prospects for someone who dreamt of setting up her own trekking establishment, as she did. We agreed that commercially horses are always a dodgy business, but I felt strongly that people should be given the opportunity of seeing the country in this way. I was by now firmly convinced that it was far the best way to travel and was already hoping that the articles, book and film about our trip would encourage others to take it up as well. A long cross-country journey such as we were undertaking did involve certain problems which were relieved by having a support vehicle. If, instead, one were to travel on hired horses around a circular route for a week or so in one of the marvellous regions of France which we had barely glimpsed as we passed through, it could make for as near to perfect a holiday as we could imagine. We had found that French farmers were generous and would allow people to camp in their fields and graze their horses. With good food and comfortable country inns everywhere there is a boundless opportunity to arrange such tours, yet most people will still prefer to stay in their cars on the crowded autoroutes.

Everyone came out to see us off and wave us goodbye. The little German girl cried and said she wanted to come with us. We felt very intrepid and romantic as we rode off northwards into the forest, leaving the rest of the party to return to M. Vergnes' house, where they would lounge by his swimming pool in the late August sunshine. We reached the ancient, pretty town of Terrasson-La-Villedieu where we had to lead the horses down the steep cobbled alleys to the Vezère river. It was market day and the stall-holders selling colourful piles of cloth, pots and pans, leatherwork, fruit and vegetables called out cheerfully to us as we rode through the traffic past the 12th-century bridge.

Out into the country beyond the railway station and some narrow lanes brought us to a jovial welcome from Roger Mallet at La Valade. The boys had already arrived and installed themselves in one of the bunkhouses where the students slept. The horses were given a field to themselves and we all had a communal supper together at which M. Mallet presided making no effort to quell the unruly mob of young people who fought over the chaotic meal which they appeared to have

LEFT Crossing the moat to arrive at Touffou.

BELOW Part of the Château Touffou.

ABOVE The Trompeurs in the hunting museum at Touffou. The retired champion horn-blower of France is in the centre with his pupil, the present champion, on the far left. Herta Ogilvy is in the centre of the back row with Solange next to her.

LEFT Michael and Serena riding across the noisy bridge over the Loire at Mauves.

BELOW A camp at dawn.

OPPOSITE The horses quickly became accustomed to traffic but . . . Tiki needed all his courage to accept a friendly lick from a cow.

ABOVE Louella inspecting the medieval carvings at Malestroit.

LEFT A picnic lunch

ABOVE Among the *menhirs* at Carnac.

LEFT A lady in Breton costume dancing at the *pardon* at Kengroix.

OVERLEAF Reflections on the Nantes–Brest Canal.

RIGHT Tiki buying bread at the *boulangerie* in Roscoff.

BELOW Thibert and Tiki choosing onions from the famous onion 'johnnie', Jean-Marie Peron.

ABOVE 'You can take a white horse anywhere': Thibert and Tiki being unloaded at Plymouth docks after crossing the Channel.

LEFT and BELOW At home at Maidenwell.

prepared themselves. Later, having transferred all the necessary information on to my own maps, I was able to return his precious ones to our host as we sat up late discussing the route ahead.

8

Through Rural France

August the 28th was Rupert's 14th birthday. One of his presents was the promise of a bicycle at his new school, King's College, Taunton, where he was due to go in a fortnight. Another was to be allowed to ride Tiki properly for the first time. While he and I tried to follow Roger Mallet's erratic orange signs across country, Louella and Jamie went to visit the splendid 10th-century Château de Hautefort, where they were impressed by the superb topiary in the gardens; the tall box hedges had been shaped into all sorts of geometrical patterns and there was one tree which had been made into a large house complete with doors and windows.

Rupert's legs were soon rubbed raw as he was not wearing boots and had not had the careful breaking-in period to which Louella and I had subjected our bodies in the Camargue. He was very brave but it was clearly painful until we hit on the idea of sliding up his trouser legs a couple of the felt pads we used under the saddles to protect the horses from saddle sores. After a long stretch through pretty woods along a well-marked grass track we came to a new and impassable wire fence across our path. There was no way round and it looked as if we would have to retrace our steps and make a detour which would add several miles to our journey. The wire cutters I had brought for just such an eventuality were not in my saddlebags that day, but had been transferred for some reason which must have made sense at the time into the tack trunk on the roof of the car. My Swiss Army knife, which had gadgets on it for almost everything, including a useful tool for taking stones out of horses' hoofs, had nothing strong enough to remove the shining new staples attaching the wire. Worried that the time for our rendezvous with Louella and Jamie had already arrived and there was still an hour's ride ahead of us, we turned back. After a few hundred yards we spotted a man gathering mushrooms on the edge of the wood. Thinking he might be the farmer who had put the fence up we rode over to ask if there was a way through. He told us that he was not responsible, but that we *should* be able to follow that track as it was a right of way and no one had a right to block it. Most kindly he laid down his basket and walked back to the fence with us. He said that the mushrooms still needed a few more days' sun to start coming up in profusion. the cèpes (boletus edulis), however, were well under way in the woods around there now. They are one of the most coveted and delicious of French edible fungi. By the time we had reached the obstruction we were firm friends and he was committed to solving our problem. Attacking the staples with his own pocket knife, he succeeded in loosening a couple and then, by jumping on the wires he brought them to the ground so that we could lead the horses over. I would never have dared smash up a fence so violently, but when I offered to help him repair it, he waved me on saying we had a long way to go and that he would make sure there was no trouble with the farmer.

We duly reached Segonzac to find Louella and Jamie waiting by a very ruined château on the edge of the village where they had spread out a delicious picnic. We turned the horses loose in the weed-covered court-yard and flopped down on the grass to tuck into lavish slices of home-cured ham, sausage and cheese sandwiched in long crusty bread. As we were finishing, an old man walked in from the village, the fumes of his midday tipple at the bar preceding him. We had not realised that the old house was occupied, as it seemed a complete ruin from the outside, the windows broken and the roof half fallen in. But he cheerfully showed us the single bare room he lived in and said we were welcome to stay as long as we liked. The owner had not been seen for years and he doubted if he would ever return now.

Rupert decided to rest his wounds during the afternoon, and so Louella and I rode on for another four hours to reach a good-looking and well-maintained château at dusk. It was called La Forge and lay across a deep valley, at the bottom of which was a huge complex of derelict buildings. Once it had been a thriving mill, the machinery driven by water from the fast-flowing Auvézère river. A wide man-made waterfall still thundered at the edge of the mill race, but the roofs were crumbling and the windows all broken. We thought of riding up the drive to the château and asking for hospitality. After all, we had a romantic tale to tell and most people should, we felt, be pleased to receive us, but our nervè failed us and we rode on to find that the boys had located a superb field with good grass and a clear running stream. As a reward, and to celebrate Rupert's birthday, we took them into Payzac where there was a small hotel in which they could have baths and sleep in beds again. We were also able to ring home from the call box in the village to find out if all was well. We learned that we had reason for a double celebration as the news had just come through that Jamie had been accepted by Aberdeen University.

Before dinner we walked across the village square to see the church, which was floodlit, although the place was practically deserted and we were the only guests in the hotel. Payzac is not mentioned in any guide books I have found, but it is a pretty place and the church was charming. Old and mellow on the outside, it had colourful stained-glass windows, domed roofs and, most strange, an aisle which bent quite sharply half-way along its length, something I have not seen before.

This corner of the Dordogne is quite different from the better-known parts where the tourists flock. It is extraordinarily quiet and peaceful with next to no traffic on the roads and few people to be seen. Occasionally we saw smart modern houses with bijou gardens and carefully laid-out rockeries; but mostly there were lovely old peasant cottages, decaying châteaux or perfect little country houses with the roofs falling in. There seemed to be very little in between these extremes. A few gleaming modern cars, their city-suited owners driving fast about their important business; local farmers in beige smocks with pitchforks or scythes working in their fields or driving very ancient tractors, and nothing in between. Almost everything is unspoilt so that the glaring modern intrusions appear all the more out of place. In the farmyards the water was still being drawn from old wells where a handle was turned to lower a bucket as the rope unwound from a rounded beam. Outside each village or hamlet there was a stone cross or sometimes a wooden one and everywhere beautifully made little slate towers popped up in unexpected places on the end of barns or in the centre of small towns. All day we had barely seen a car on the country roads when we had chosen to follow them rather than attempt to cut across country; perhaps one car an hour passed us. It was quite hilly country, green and lush but not very productive as the slopes were too steep for intensive cultivation. We saw almost no flat land and in many places there were undrained rushy meadows cut by streams and bordered by forests of oak and sweet chestnut. It had been very peaceful and still, a hot sultry day with a haze so that we could not see far when we reached the top of each hill.

During the afternoon we stopped to water the horses at a rainwater trough in a delightfully ramshackle farmyard. Two very old ladies and an equally elderly man came out to ask us where we were headed. They expressed extreme amazement when they heard we were going all the way to England and said that it must be very hard especially on 'Madame'. When I said that I, too, was a farmer and that the horses were for work at home, they were most interested and they questioned me closely about the sort of farming we practised in Cornwall. They told us theirs was a very mixed farm with a little bit of everything; some pigs, some cows, sheep, goats, chickens, ducks, geese, guinea fowl and rabbits; some vines, some potatoes, fruit trees, vegetables, corn and maize.

'It must be very hard work,' I said, 'no peace at any time of the year.' They agreed vigorously that it was a hard life and that, they said, was why the young people would no longer tolerate it.

That night we feasted on the set menu, the rough house wine being thrown in free, as much as we could drink. A plain cake with a single candle was brought in to mark Rupert's birthday and afterwards we all played Scrabble until much too late.

We were woken early by a dreadful cacophony of competitive village cocks crowing madly from about five but still made a late start after a leisurely breakfast of croissants and hot chocolate. The country became more gentle and rolling with apple orchards and dairy cows; plenty of pleasant woods to ride through too, where the trees shaded us from the heat of the sun. Only the dogs disturbed the peace and they were a feature of riding across France with which we were by now quite familiar. The French are very different from the British in their approach to dogs. Perhaps it is due to their fear of being burgled or perhaps they represent a form of status symbol, but almost every house in the country or in the suburbs of towns has at least one dog and almost without exception they appear to spend their entire lives tied up. On every gate there is a sign saying *Chien méchant*, a notice which does not vary in emphasis whether the guardian of the house is a clearly very *méchant*, even mad wretch of an Alsatian, its eyes glaring as it froths at the mouth and strains at its chain, or whether it is a tiny papillon which minces up to the gate screaming high-pitched abuse. Hounds and terriers of all shapes and sizes add their varying bays and yaps to the chorus, and in this region we often saw extraordinary-looking dogs which I took to be truffle hounds. They had rough coats and wagged their tails furiously in a circle while emitting hoarse gasps as they strained on their leashes. None of these unfortunates seemed ever to be taken for a walk and many were a cruel sight as they paced up and down in a desperately confined area or lay chained up in their own filth. Almost the only truly healthy happy dogs we saw were those being worked by farmers to round up sheep or cattle. The rest seemed by our standards to lead a woefully dreary existence. We comforted ourselves by concluding that at least our arrival brought some interest into their lives since horses were not often to be seen on the roads.

It was as we approached the outskirts of towns that the fun really began. The first guard dog we met would set off a chain reaction which we could hear being picked up all along the street and away into the distance. Soon there would be bedlam as in one garden after another what seemed to be whole packs of dogs would hurl themselves at the fence or charge to the end of their chains only to be jerked violently back time after time until we felt they surely must break their necks. Cats fled for the rooftops, and windows were flung open as the owners shouted at their pets to shut up, while we clipped-clopped blithely past conscious that we could hardly be blamed for all the fuss we were creating and only hoping that the chains and fences would hold.

In the early afternoon we rode up from the deep green valley of the Isle river to the impressive château of Jumilhac-le-Grand built on a rocky spur. The roofs, towers and turrets bore a mass of decoration – lead figurines holding tridents, weathercocks, ornate tiles and fantastic embellishments. It all seemed in very good condition and appeared to be lived in. As we rounded the corner to approach the main gates we found a neat rectangular town laid out, the large tree-lined central square facing the château. A circus had arrived and men were working hard through the heat of the afternoon to erect the tents and funfairs, dodgems and merry-go-rounds. Across the square was an inviting restaurant with tables on the pavement protected by large umbrellas. We rode over, dismounted, and tied the horses to the shutter hooks of the next house along. Sitting at the end table we called for cold drinks and a large plate of charcuterie. The waiter, determinedly refusing to manifest any surprise, brought us what we ordered and studiously ignored the horses, as did the other guests eating at the next table. The enjoyment of good food is such a serious business in France that we often found that our arrival, with all the inevitable disruption we caused, unsaddling the horses, tying them up and borrowing a bucket to bring them water from a tap in the kitchen, was not allowed to distract anyone from the matter in hand until the meal was over. Then everyone would come to pat Thibert and Tiki and ask us all about our journey. We learned that the château was indeed still in private hands and that Madame la Comtesse did occasionally come and stay there.

After a long, hard day spent on country roads which climbed steeply up and down narrow valleys, we came on another, but quite different château, Montbrun, just as the sun was setting. Its round crenellated towers were reflected in a deep moat reminding me of Leeds Castle in Kent. It had an extraordinarily English feel to it, accentuated by the fine trees surrounding it, the two horses, one white one black, grazing the edge of the moat and the imposing gentleman in cavalry-twill trousers, the owner I assumed, who was strolling with his family on the lawn. As we rode past in the evening stillness, Louella commented on the familiarity of it all and I saw heads turn as her voice carried across the water. I could not resist answering loudly, 'Of course it looks English. We must have built it when this was all part of England.'

In fact I was not only being provocative but also inaccurate, I later learned, as it was one of the few fortresses which had managed to hold out against Richard Coeur de Lion when he laid siege to it in 1199.

Soon after, we met Rupert and Jamie, who had found a good field nearby where we could all camp. As they had already eaten, we drove off to Châlus leaving them to feed and rub down the horses while we had some dinner. We paid a quick visit to the remains of the old château high above the centre of the town. This was where King Richard, after failing to reduce the Château de Montbrun, came in search of a great hoard of gold which was hidden at Châlus. As he directed the siege, thinking he was well out of range of the defenders' arrows, he was struck in the shoulder by the bolt from a new and more powerful type of crossbow, a sort of secret weapon. It was this wound which, brushed aside at the time as a mere scratch, was to fester and finally kill the 42-year-old king at Chinon some days later. When the siege was broken all the defenders were hanged – except for the unfortunate, accurate and inventive crossbowman who was burnt alive.

We returned to the field well after dark to sling our hammocks between the roof-rack and a tree by torchlight. There was a murky pond from which Rupert kindly fetched us water to wash and brush our teeth in. Louella's bucket had a frog in it. In spite of that we all slept soundly.

For the next three days we headed north fast, crossing the Vienne for the first time where it still flowed to the west across our route, then again at Confolens after it had turned to run due north. We were anxious to reach our next resting place where we were also due to do some more filming with the BBC. This was all planned to happen at Touffou, the beautiful château owned and lived in by Louella's cousin David Ogilvy. David and his wife Herta had invited us to stay and rest ourselves and the horses at what was just about the half-way point on our journey. We had stayed with them the year before and were looking forward to the luxury of a four-poster bed and a few days of relative peace. But to get there on time meant pushing ourselves and the horses hard and resisting almost every temptation to tarry on the way.

On the first day, however, we went so far that in the end it was no problem. We did this by sticking firmly to roads on which we could not get lost and keeping going hour after hour, often at the uncomfortable trot which neither we nor the horses particularly enjoyed, but which did cover the ground at a very satisfactory average speed. That day we covered about 60 km to reach Confolens in just under 10 hours and that evening we were both fairly stiff for the first time.

Two buildings stand out in memory from that day's ride. One was the most peculiar twisted church spire in Rochechouart. It struck us as a remarkable technical achievement, the small slates neatly fitted together to lead the eye upwards and around in a delightful way. There was no reference to it in the guide book. Instead there was a charming story attached to the fine castle which now houses the municipal offices as well as a museum. It seems that in 1205 the Vicomte Aymeric de Rochechouart married a woman of such beauty that everyone fell for her, including the Vicomte's steward. Unable to seduce her, he went to his master and said that she had made amorous advances to him. Mad with jealousy the Vicomte ordered that his wife should be fed to a ravenous lion which he happened to have in the East tower. After two days he went to look at the lion and found it asleep at his undamaged wife's feet. Her innocence being thus self-evident the truth came out and the steward took her place. This time the lion showed more appetite.

The other building which enchanted us that day was the small Château de Rochebrune. Here again there was the feel of an English country house as, in spite of the four round towers reflected in the moat, there was nothing formidable about it. We could see into the central courtyard where there was a tennis court and a row of children's clothes of varying sizes hanging on a washing line. So many of the châteaux and fine houses we had seen were either being allowed to fall down or had been made into museums or offices that it always came as a relief to see one that was being lived in and loved.

Beyond was the great Forêt d'Etagnac. Here we saw lots of red squirrels. They seemed smaller than those I remember from my youth before they were driven out by the greys, and had white patches underneath. All along the road the trees bore notices saying CHASSE GARDÉE, although it seemed to us that such a huge forest would be very hard to police. In some of the regions we passed through notices about shooting were plastered over the trees in such profusion that they became a positive blot on the landscape. There were many variations on the general theme: CHASSE PRIVÉE, CHASSE INTERDITE, RESERVE DE CHASSE, DEFENSE D'ENTRER, PROPRIÉTÉ PRIVÉ, sometimes on almost every tree. My favourite was one put up by a commune which declared that no partridges whatsoever were to be shot in that district – except on Sunday 9 October. Clearly that was a day to keep one's head well down. In other regions there were no notices at all and, if anything, there seemed to be more birds around in those.

Apart from those notices about shooting, one of the best things about the French countryside is that so much of it feels uncontaminated by man. Having spent my childhood in Ireland, I remember being quite shocked when I first went to England and found so much of the country sullied in some way. In *real* country you would never find a tin can or bottle under the hedges. Although in France some of the suburbs of the towns are as squalid as anywhere and some villages are positively medieval in their approach to rubbish and effluent disposal, once out in the country it feels much freer and less spoiled than Britain in certain significant ways. This may be because the population density overall in France is only about 250 people to the square mile, while it is over 900 in England (and just over 100 in Ireland). Perhaps also it has something to do with the French passion for gathering things in their countryside. Almost everyone takes the time to search for mushrooms and other diverse fungi, nuts and fruit in their season, not to mention all the birds, animals and fish which are compulsively pursued. Although this leads to excessive and shameful over-hunting of birds, for example, it may also encourage a stronger interest in preserving the countryside, since so many derive pleasure and food from it.

As we emerged from the forest we looked into a farmyard and glimpsed a scene which must have barely changed for a century or more. An old couple dressed in shapeless smocks led a sturdy white carthorse drawing a high-sided wooden cart stacked with plump marrows. Their hands were gnarled and their backs bowed as they drew up beside a half-timbered shed with mud and wattle walls where they began slowly to lift the marrows off the cart and stack them. In this region we seldom saw young people working the land. It was still fairly poor country with small rushy fields where white milch cows dappled with brown spots grazed and flocks of small sheep with pink snub noses like pigs were watched over by old men. In the orchards mistletoe hung so profusely from the trees that it was sometimes impossible to see whether there were fruit or not. Parasitic plants like mistletoe and mosses are among the most sensitive indicators of pollution levels in the atmosphere. The Christmas after our return to England there was a shortage of mistletoe in the shops and it was announced that what there was had largely been imported from France so that the price had shot up.

Once we were on the left bank of the Vienne the country gradually became richer and had a more prosperous feel to it. The farming units were larger, growing extensive crops of maize and sunflowers. The fields were bigger, houses grander with regular châteaux and some interesting fortified farms as well as modern intrusions like factories and housing estates seen in the distance. The views over the Vienne were often breathtaking, especially in the early morning when the mist rose from the water clothing the tall poplars as far as their highest branches.

Lunching on the terrace of the Hôtel du Barrage opposite L'Isle Jourdain (32 francs for five courses including ham and eggs followed by steak and chips) we put the horses to graze in the small sloping garden by the river. We watched anxiously as they decided to roll, something they nearly always did when unsaddled, and breathed a sigh of relief as they neatly passed between the pots of flowering geraniums to end up against the retaining wall. They then decided to join us on the terrace and had to be led firmly back to the grass. The management were extraordinarily tolerant.

The boys found a succession of small fields on the river bank from which they could bathe in the rather muddy waters of the Vienne. These last days of August were so scorchingly hot that we were tempted to join them but all the hard riding we were doing made the prospect of a hot bath even more attractive and we tended to hurry to a hotel in the evenings leaving them to camp. At dawn we would find Jamie sitting quietly writing up his journal in the early-morning mist while the horses grazed next to him. Rupert, still inside his bright red sleeping bag, rolled about on the ground before crawling out and pretending to be busy. We brought them hot chocolate and buns from our hotel, saddled up and mounted to leave them to clear up the camp and laze by the river until our next rendezvous. They did not have a bad time.

There were noticeably less water troughs and village fountains now and, in spite of the big river which was usually in sight but inaccessible, we had difficulty watering the horses as often as we would have wished on those hot days. In Queaux there was a series of excellent public washing troughs where the water gushed in profusion from a natural spring. Here the horses could drink deeply next to the wooden scrubbing boards neatly lined up on the edge ready for the next washday. Another time we stopped at a smart little modern house where the water from the pond in the garden poured over a wall into a grating in the road. Tiki drank from the flow, but Thibert found this impossible and shook his head violently, splashing us all but getting none in his mouth. The kind couple who lived there were amused and brought a bucket to make it easier for him. They also brought glasses of cold water for us, and we talked. When we told them that we were going to stay with my wife's cousin at Touffou in a couple of days they told us with pride that their families had worked as domestics for the old Count from whom David had bought the château, and they clearly regarded this connection as superior to our own.

It was on the banks of the Vienne that we met the only other real *randonneurs equestres* we were to see on our whole journey. Just after passing Moussac, a village on the far bank of the Vienne, we came to a house where a pack of good-looking foxhounds set up an exceptionally loud chorus of welcome as we passed. We assumed that it was a hunt kennel and so were not surprised to see three people approaching on fine horses. We stopped to give our horses a drink from a stream which crossed the road at that point and they joined us: a smartly turned-out man and woman on two big chestnut mares and another man on a black gelding whom we took at first to be hunt servants. But they told us that they had ridden over from Usson-du-Poitou some 15 km to the west and that they were regular *randonneurs*, sometimes travelling for up to a month at a time away from home. In all the years they had been doing this we were the first other *randonneurs* they had ever met. We were interested in seeing that they had saddlebags just like ours and a map case identical to the old British army one which my father-in-law had lent us. However, they were using English hunting saddles and wore breeches and polished riding boots. They were very friendly and invited us back to their place where they said they had good stables and facilities for horses. We thanked them but said we had to hurry on to Touffou.

That evening the journey nearly came to an end for Tiki. The riverside field which the boys had borrowed was bounded by a rather broken-down wire fence. This would not normally have mattered as both horses were good about not trying to escape and had a great respect for electric fences so that even one strand of wire with no current through it was enough to keep them in. This time, though, there was a herd of cows in the next field and across the road inland a diminutive grey stallion clearly thought our horses were interesting mares and was making an almighty racket, squealing and racing up and down. Now the odd thing was that Thibert and Tiki, in spite of being bred for work with bulls and coming from the Camargue where they must have spent their lives next to cattle, were both scared stiff of cows. We had made a point of trying to break this fear, but when this unknown herd rushed towards them just after they had been unsaddled and released, they panicked. Taking off at full gallop towards the frantically whinnying stallion, who presumably represented equine security, they failed to notice the wire fence and crashed through it. Thibert carried on but Tiki was stopped by the wire which wrapped itself round one of his hind legs. It was one of those moments when the whole scenario of a major disaster flashed through my mind. If Tiki broke a leg he would have to be shot. Would I then carry on alone on Thibert? Could we return to the Camargue and fetch a replacement for Louella? Would we have to call the whole thing off?

We all ran across the field, slowed down as we neared Tiki and walked towards him talking soothingly. Sensibly he stopped struggling and allowed us to remove the wire. Thibert had meanwhile come back to join his friend, who had so unaccountably stopped in mid flight, and allowed himself to be caught. We led them over to the stallion, who continued to squeal hysterically but got the message that they were not mares, returned them to their field, repaired the fence and at last settled them down for the night.

The night before we were due to arrive at Touffou we sampled the hotel in Chauvigny into which we had booked the British BBC crew who were about to join us. For once we were expected, as we had written ahead and one of our fliers was pinned up in Reception. Madame positively simpered as we checked in. The combination of our fame and the large amount of custom we were bringing meant that we could do no wrong in her eyes. Since we only had a short distance to ride and had said we would arrive at Touffou after lunch we were able to have a rare lie-in that Sunday morning. We watched a strange sight from our bedroom window. A large French family also staying in the hotel were assembling across the courtyard to go into breakfast. The mother was dominating and the children boisterous but at last they left in the direction of the dining room. The father, a nervous and rather furtive man, then emerged with a small black cat on a lead. For half an hour he walked patiently up and down beside the flowerbeds as the little cat gambolled round him, rolling on its back and playing with its lead but never doing what was intended. He was still there when we went into breakfast ourselves to find the rest of his family eating heartily and patently satisfied that all was well with the world.

9

Touffou

The boys were valiantly scrubbing the horses so that they would look smart for our arrival at Touffou. They had borrowed a hosepipe from the kind farmer, M. Ribereau, whose field we were using, and had been allowed to run it through the vegetable patch of a neighbour. The Ribereaux were simple people who had worked this piece of land all their lives and were now worried about the future as his back was giving out and they had no son to carry on. They were hospitality itself and Madame said that we must not leave without sampling her special home-made Crème de Cassis. This is usually drunk as a splash to which a glass of white wine is added, making the delicious 'kir' which we enjoyed everywhere in France; it is named after a former mayor of Dijon and Resistance hero Canon Félix Kir who popularised the drink. Madame poured us each a small glass of the thick blackcurrant syrup, but as it is slightly alcoholic she considered Rupert too young to have any. She and her husband then rose to their feet and raised their glasses to us as we took our first sip of the exquisite nectar. Such grace and good manners were often displayed by French peasant farmers we met and it was moments like that which for all of us transcended the need to be fluent in each other's languages. I was at the time reading Laurens van der Post's *Yet Being Someone Other*, in which he describes how extraordinarily close people of quite different cultural backgrounds can become, even without any means of verbal communication. 'It was my first intimation that human beings communicate in a way far more profoundly with one another through the nature of what they are, than through their words.' In just the same way we were made to feel honoured guests and old friends by people in whose debt we already were through having been given free grazing.

With the horses gleaming white we rode slowly along the remaining stretch of the Vienne before Touffou, careful not to work them up into a lather. Here a succession of fishing huts lined the bank. Each tiny shed has a small lawn beside it running down to the water where the family can gather for a picnic at the weekend and watch papa demonstrate his skill with a rod. Few of these huts looked as though they were intended for staying in overnight but many of the gardens were carefully tended, with fruit trees and flowering shrubs. To English eyes they were a novel form of country cottage.

At last the moment of our arrival at Touffou was upon us. It is the most beautiful château I know anywhere. The evening before we had driven Rupert and Jamie up for a sneak preview. Seen from across the river, rising out of the dusky mist it is the ultimate fairy castle. Its great towers, roofed in blue-black slate, rise above a rampart wall lining the river bank. Behind them is the beautiful façade of the Renaissance building while surmounting everything is the massive *donjon* or keep which was built and occupied before the Norman Conquest. The château is David's passion and he has lavished a fortune on it. As the founder and Chairman of Ogilvy, Benson and Mather, a living legend in the advertising world, he is still a most powerful and formidable man at 72. Feared by many for his intolerance of fools and his ability to be exceedingly rude if it suits him, he fortunately adores Louella who is not afraid of him and can usually get away with answering him back in kind. His devastating good looks and the charm with which he can reduce any girl to jelly, have not deserted him but while with him there is always the added spice of a potential rage just around the corner. We call him *le sanglier*, the wild boar.

Making sure everything was clean, tidy and in its place we set off up the long drive towards the château. We were being watched for and with perfect timing the bell began to peal as we approached. All the family and friends who were staying poured out into the courtyard and we were given a tremendous welcome. It was a scene which was to be repeated several times over the next few days as the BBC, who had not by then arrived, tried to recapture it on film. That first time, at least, our joy and relief to have reached the half-way point were genuine as we were hugged and kissed and had our hands shaken by everyone. David's beautiful wife Herta, a consummate hostess with a wicked sense of humour which makes her a perfect foil for him, took us to our old room and for the first time since setting out we were able to unpack completely and have all our dirty clothes washed. For the next three days we could relax and enjoy ourselves.

The walls of Touffou are a delicate soft apricot in the hot sunlight, a most unusual and restful colour. David decided to remove the ancient ivy from the wall above the dry moat (where wild boar were once kept) and we helped him. It was hard work as each tendril clung tenaciously but the enthusiasm with which he told us about his beloved château made the time fly. He plays with the colossal unified set of ancient buildings which make up the château like a child arranging a dolls house.

He has restored it without diminishing it as so often happens when either money is skimped or bold endeavours shirked. The roofs were in bad repair when he acquired it twenty years ago from the previous owner Comte Enguerand de Vergie. Instead of picking out the worst and trying to save them, he has had the whole lot restored and rebuilt over the last few years, a task which has cost £4 million, to which the French government have contributed half. Now it seems nearly perfect and finished, but David still has plans and he is never at rest. The ivy, we realise, is being removed so that Touffou will look its best for the BBC. As we work he points out the twelve fine orange trees in square white tubs placed around the courtyard. These have to be carried, as they always have been, like sedan chairs into the orangery in October each year as the nights grow cold. But the courtyard looks bare without them and so he has had twelve more tubs made in which evergreen bushes are grown which can survive the winter and which in their turn are hidden during the summer.

I told David that we had run out of feed for the horses and that we would be buying more in the morning. I wondered if I could find some in the château's stables to give them that day. We put down our trowels and went in search. The Comte de Vergie was a great master of hounds. Indeed he ran his own pack from Touffou and the field were always all his guests. In the château is a large hunting museum, which includes an extensive collection of hunt buttons from France and England. The stables are in keeping and we went from rows of spacious stalls to empty quarters for grooms and stable boys. Up creaking stairways there were lofts and into these we peered with David questing determinedly, sure that there was feed somewhere. For a moment when a light bulb failed to light there was a rumble and I thought the *sanglier* would erupt, then in the dark we felt a big pile of oats and we filled a bucket.

Thibert and Tiki were in a beautiful paddock with a white post-and-rail fence alongside the river. They were down by the river drinking but cantered over when I called, and ate the uncrushed oats happily.

Rupert stayed with us in the château. There seemed an endless crowd of young who came and went, some staying, some visiting. Herta's children by a previous marriage to Comte Bernard Claret de la Touche, whose own château lay half a day's ride away, were all there. Guy, who was at Atlantic College, had friends of diverse nationalities staying for the holidays, as is the custom with students there. Isabelle and Minouche, her daughters, also had friends staying and Minouche planned to ride with us to her father's when we left. I was glad to see Rupert mixing with young people who switched languages as easily as expressions. British children take such a long time to stop being self-conscious about this. I know I did.

Jamie stayed in Chauvigny where his girlfriend Alex was due to arrive at the same time as the BBC. She was going to take over as his helper from Rupert, who had to go back to school in a few days. That first night at Touffou, twenty-one of us dined by candlelight under the stars on the terrace over the Vienne. It was warm, still and summery. It had not rained for two months and when I said we should enjoy it while it lasted, everyone laughed saying there was no sign whatever of a change. 'Wait and see what happens tomorrow,' I said. Howard had still not arrived and we discussed the filming he wanted to do with David and Herta. We were all a bit nervous about how David would react to the crew and especially how he would get on with Howard. We need not have worried. They saw eye to eye at once when they met the next day and David even agreed to take part, showing Louella and me around Touffou and telling us something about the château on film. Working with him was an eye-opener. We had become rather pleased with ourselves, thinking we were pretty good in front of the camera at delivering our lines and acting natural. David showed us how it should be done. He is a natural performer with perfect timing and great experience. In fact he admitted that he should really have been an actor like his nephew Ian.

'If I had been,' he said immodestly, 'I would have been knighted by now. But they don't give knighthoods to advertising men!'

We started with some interior scenes. When it came to David's first bit of talk, telling us about the great beamed salon in the *donjon*, the cameraman said we had better wait while he changed the reel as there were only two and a half minutes left. 'That's just enough,' said David, and on cue launched into a fluent description of its history and how some years ago he had held a ball there and worried that the ceiling would fall in with all the dancers. 'When it hadn't collapsed by four a.m. I went to bed,' he finished, turned and said, 'that should be enough,' and the cameraman exclaimed, 'My God, he's exactly right.'

We simply smiled, nodded and tagged along as David performed for the camera. At one of the grand pianos he sat down and was filmed, as he said he had always wanted to be, playing a Beethoven Piano Concerto superbly, only to get up and walk away in the middle while the music played on from the concealed gramophone. In the St Johns tower where King Francis I (1515–47) was reputed to have stayed, we wanted to film the high-vaulted ceiling covered in frescoes done in the 17th century by an itinerant painter in the style of the Venetian Bassano brothers. They depict scenes of the four seasons and are like crude but lively versions of the *Très Riches Heures du Duc de Berry*. Louella put Howard up to daring to suggest as a joke that David should lie flat on the floor looking upwards when describing them to us. Without a hesitation he was down there and that was how we were all filmed.

Poor Howard. While this was all going on happily indoors, the skies opened and it began to pour down outside. Everyone at Touffou was amazed as there had been no warning; the heatwave and drought were expected to last much longer. It was particularly unfortunate as most of the rest of the scenes planned for filming at Touffou were outdoors. The first was to have been a grand luncheon party on the terrace. During the morning the table had been laid *en fête* with flowers and specially folded napkins. In an instant everything was soaked and we all rushed to carry it in. In the afternoon it cleared up a bit and we decided to risk filming our arrival. Everyone was assembled in the courtyard and on the steps of the château stood seven French hunting-horn players. These are serious musical instruments and indeed stag-hunting in France is as much a matter of music as it is of sport. David took on with the château the champion horn-blower of France who, having retired as head groom, until quite recently still blew a morning fanfare to awaken everyone. He was there to watch, and among the group immaculately turned out in their green hunt livery was the new Champion of France, a pupil of the old man's. Because they are circular, winding around several times on themselves, these horns are blown with the blowers facing away from the listeners; the highly polished flaring trumpet end emerges backwards under the player's elbow.

Inevitably as we cantered flamboyantly through the gates the rain came down again and the crowd fled. Only the horn-players stood their ground and together made an opening burst of sound so loud and unexpected that both Thibert and Tiki shied violently sideways and almost jumped into the moat. While we returned the horses to their field, Herta took charge, lit a huge fire in the hunting museum, produced quantities of mulled wine and moved everyone in there. It was a splendid setting for filming; the stags' antlers around the walls, the strange acoustics of the hall, the steaming hunt coats of the red-faced players as the fire lifted the rainwater from them, all conspired to give a wonderful effect.

The sound was deafeningly loud at first, and Ed the BBC sound recordist hunched miserably inside his earphones, wincing visibly. But then our ears became attuned and the rich, primitive noise with its simple melody took us over. The *trompeurs* faced into the blazing fireplace from which the crackle and roar of the dry brushwood added a background percussion. As we watched, listened and filmed, applauding their backs between numbers, they played a series of traditional tunes for us, including one called Touffou, which was always played at the château before the hunt moved off. Howard was pleased and we posed happily after a successful filming session.

One of the players was a neighbour and friend of David and Herta called Solange, who had an antique shop in Bonneuil-Matours. She was glamorous and vivacious, giving just that risqué touch which is so often found in the hunting field. She stayed to dinner, exotic in her riding habit, and afterwards sang some more of the hunting songs for us in a rich contralto with theatrical accompanying gestures.

The horses' shoes were again worn paper-thin and Herta arranged for a blacksmith to call. There is a shortage of blacksmiths in Poitou, surprising as it is a popular riding area and several hunts still survive; there was no hot forge available. Instead a man came who could put on shoes cold. He was not a real blacksmith but we were lucky to get anyone and he did a fair job in the end. He was quite rough with the horses and Tiki did not like him at all. He was fat and rather loud-mouthed and every time he lifted one of Tiki's feet Tiki reared up to try and escape. In the end we had to put on Tiki's upper lip a 'twitch', a noose which is tightened by a twisting stick attached to it, to restrain him. This is something I prefer not to do if at all possible but it worked, although Tiki looked at us most reproachfully thereafter. The fat man also said Tiki was seven years old, had had infected feet, currently had worms and would never make it to England. This was worrying as others en route had suggested he might be older than the four and a half years we had been assured by his owner in the Camargue. Minouche and I pored over a book of hers which explained the peculiar way in which a horse's age can be deduced from its teeth and reckoned he really was only four, but it is hard to be sure unless you are an expert. Both horses had been wormed before departure, but to be on the safe side we sent Jamie to buy some more doses and give them to them that evening. Tiki was now fully recovered from the after-effects of strangles and, though still thin, seemed to us full of beans, which only made the blacksmith's gloom more annoying. Thibert had developed another cold so that his nose ran fairly constantly and I was giving him another course of penicillin injections, but he too looked to us better and stronger than ever. In fact the château oats we had been giving them during their rest had made them thoroughly frisky, so that when the BBC again tried to film a staged arrival, they performed with panache. The sun shone briefly, the château glowed, everyone cheered and at last all went well.

Howard wanted to film a scene in which we set up camp and slept in our hammocks. This would, he felt, give good material for a natural break between episodes. There was a good spot in the orchard behind the château where we could drive the car close to an old tree dripping with ripe apples. With our hammocks tied between the tree trunk and the roofrack we were filmed on our last evening at Touffou first waking up, plucking our breakfast from a branch above our heads and stepping out barefoot in our night things to wake the boys. Jamie was in the tent nearby and emerged cheerfully to greet the supposed dawn. Rupert, curled up in his red sleeping bag outside, simply grunted and rolled over as usual as I kicked him. The horses, who were standing nearby watching our antics in some amazement, accepted apples from us and stood resignedly as, having just been unsaddled after the final 'arrival' scene, we pretended to get them ready for another long day.

Luckily there was a glorious sunset so that, returning to our hammocks, we could then be filmed lying in the fading light with an orange backcloth as I spoke into my miniature tape recorder about how we hoped to arrive at Touffou and sleep in a big four-poster the next day while Louella, in her hammock alongside, wrote up her journal.

As we packed up to return to the château a perfect rainbow reached out from behind the *donjon* over the St John's tower and down to the river beyond. No time to set up cameras or mount horses and ride into shot, it was a moment simply to be enjoyed; the best works of man and nature in perfect harmony for once.

10

Châteaux and Wine

A hazy autumnal morning for our departure from Touffou: as we rode out early through the gates, the deep cut of the Vienne was filled from bank to bank with mist and only the fine arched bridge in the distance showed. Minouche was with us and we none of us looked back. Knowing all that apricot beauty was behind us was memory enough.

For an hour we sped along country tracks which Minouche, riding between us on her beloved Kiki, knew. She told us there was an excellent patisserie in Bonneuil-Matours and so, having left before breakfast, we stopped in the charming tree-lined central square. Solange came out to see us with her daughter Emeraude. Two more beautiful little girls, Fleur and Diane, appeared and the three of them climbed on and off Thibert and Tiki who stood patiently while they were made a fuss of. M. Choquet, the baker in his white coat, was delighted to see us and brought out his finest home-made biscuits for us to sample. We seemed to have all the time in the world until, soon after, we became hopelessly lost on an unmarked road through a huge forest. We came out at the large, grim and apparently deserted Château de Fou. It was badly damaged during the war and David had told us the story of how this happened. For a time the German High Command had been billeted at Touffou. Finding this out from the Resistance, it was presumably decided by the British War Cabinet that this was too good a chance to miss and an RAF plane was despatched to bomb them out of existence. However the pilot misunderstood his instructions or read his map wrong and dropped his bombs on the similarly named Le Fou which has never fully recovered. His mistake may for all I know have prolonged the war, but I cannot help being pleased that he made it and that Touffou was spared.

Another couple of hours roadwork, during which we had to cross the main Paris–Bordeaux road, the M10, where the lorries and cars thundered past with barely a break, and then mercifully by a bridge over the autoroute, the A10 (l'Aquitaine), and we reached our rendezvous with Minouche's brother Guy. We had arranged to meet at Le Manoir de La Massardière, one of the most perfect medieval manor houses in France, which their father had sold a few years before. We posed in front of it for a photograph and I asked Guy if he was not unhappy that such a beautiful property should have gone out of his family. 'It is lovely, but quite impossible to live in,' he replied cheerfully.

We followed him across country as he drove his mother's yellow Volkswagen over ploughed fields and up a muddy lane to reach La Gatinalière, the smaller and rather more manageable château where his father now lives. It is approached by a fine avenue of mature lime trees up which we cantered three abreast. We clattered up to the terrace in the centre of the façade, scattering gravel on to the flowerbeds and frightening the horses in the paddock alongside. Once again, in spite of our unmannerly behaviour, which we blamed on our desire to behave like medieval troubadours, and although we had not previously met, Guy's father Bernard greeted us amiably and we all sat down to a delicious picnic lunch which his eldest daughter Isabel had prepared, having driven over from Touffou. With the picnic we all drank several bottles of Prince Pirate, a claret which I have sometimes bought in England. Isabelle explained how its name conceals its origin which is the anonymous surplus of some of the great Bordeaux vineyards. Hence it can sometimes be quite wonderful, although you never know what you are drinking until you open the bottle.

Guy helped us to work out our route ahead to Richelieu, which we planned to reach that night. He also told me that the French *départements* were originally planned on the basis that it should be no more than one day's hard ride, or about 80 km from the chief town or village to the frontier with the next *départements* in all directions. In this way the authorities could keep daily control from the centre, if necessary.

We still had nearly 30 km to go and so we thanked Bernard, said goodbye to everyone and left. Minouche and Kiki were to stay the night with her father and ride back to Touffou the next day. We had decided to follow the main road instead of trying to go across country. It ran dead straight for mile after mile and the heavy traffic sped along it at a tremendous speed. Fortunately there was a good wide verge along which we could canter slowly, while at the same time eating up the distance without any possibility of getting lost. For a time the film crew drove alongside us filming through their car's open window. Then they went ahead to wait and, using their longest lens, achieved some extraordinary effects as we cantered straight towards them, slowly emerging from dips in the road which stretched away behind us to the horizon.

Richelieu is a unique town. It was built from scratch by the Cardinal on a perfect rectangular plan with decorated gateways, walls and a moat. To the south lies the huge Park which used to contain a marvellous palace filled with works of art as well as fine sculptures, including

Michelangelo's *The Slaves*, obelisks, formal gardens and long straight avenues of chestnut and plane trees leading to pavilions and orangeries. All the treasures were removed at the time of the Revolution but the Park remains and we rode in through a side gate, hoping thereby to avoid riding through the town. The friends with whom Herta had arranged for us to stay, and about whom we knew nothing save for their name and business, had a house which bordered the Park on the far side and there was supposed to be a gate through which we could enter their garden. We felt very grand riding along with vistas leading away to fine buildings on all sides but the place seemed deserted and we began to wonder if we were trespassing. There were pheasants everywhere which seemed quite tame and we concluded that, since the whole thousand acres and more of the Park was contained within a high wall, it was one of the few places in France where game could effectively be reared without being poached. It was almost a relief when a car drew up and a man who introduced himself as the Gamekeeper got out, asked us if we realised that this was *propriété privé* and said that there was no way through. Since it was by now a very long way round and getting late we exerted all the charm we could raise and threw ourselves on his mercy. The poor horses, we told him, had come all the way from the Camargue and were exhausted; our good friend Bruno de Croutte, the well-known builder of swimming pools, of whom he had doubtless heard, was waiting anxiously for us beyond his garden gate; surely someone with such an important job as his would be able to help us. At last he melted and said that yes there was a secret locked way into the town and he would let us through that. We followed his car and were released into the busy main street. Down this we rode admiring the well-preserved buildings on either side. The fine hôtels with white stone decorations were designed to house the nobility who had lived there when it became, as intended, the capital of France. Like modern Brasilia, Richelieu had placed his principality in the geographical centre of the country. Off to the side led smaller but equally unspoiled streets where some of his 1,300 servants were housed.

Leaving by a gateway in the north-east corner of the town, we followed the Park wall until we came to the de Croutte house. This, a delightfully eccentric 'Edwardian' château, was reputed once to have been the town brothel. Now it was owned by the generous de Crouttes who allowed Alex and the boys to camp in the garden while the horses grazed there. The only problem was the large swimming pool. I felt sure that the horses would amble into it during the night and drown. Obligingly Bruno de Croutte dug out an electric fence from the potting shed and as darkness fell we erected it. We stayed in the appropriately named Hôtel Le Faisan, our room overlooking the elegant Place du Marché and the classical white front of the church of Notre Dame. The bill came to 60 francs, or £2.50 each for the night.

I awoke with a start. This was the day on which Michael Sissons, my literary agent, and Serena Davies were due to fly out and relieve us while we went home to see that all was well and to put Rupert into his new school. We would be away for four days during which Jamie and Alex would look after them and they would ride along the Loire. Jamie was to fetch them from the airport at Nantes but I had not worked out how far away that was, optimistically imagining that the drive should not take him more than an hour. While asleep my subconscious had been working and I woke up suspecting that it would take more than twice that, a fact confirmed by a quick glance at the map. Jamie should have left already. It is bad for the nerves to start the day in a rush and I was thoroughly scratchy by the time I had rung the de Crouttes to ask them to send Jamie at once to fetch us since he had the car in the garden; then telephoned Air France in Nantes to deliver a message for Michael saying that we would be late. We packed up, bought flowers for Madame de Croutte, saddled the horses and set off. It had taken a long time to find the horses as they had wandered off into the woods bordering the Park and when I mounted Thibert I realised that for the first time on the ride he was distinctly lame, favouring his off fore leg. There was some heat and my temper was not improved by the moral dilemma I had to resolve as to whether to ignore all my instincts and carry on regardless, or complicate everyone else's life dreadfully by insisting that Thibert have a day's rest. Trusting in the Camargue horses' reputation for toughness, I decided to carry on. Once back on the road, clip-clopping along the verge it was hard to stay cross and I calmed down. Throughout, Louella and Rupert, who was to be picked up by the BBC from the de Crouttes (another telephone call) while Alex went with Jamie, had quietly carried on with what had to be done, leaving me to rant and rage.

On our way we would pass the Sainte-Chapelle in Champigny-sur-Veude. It was Herta who had said that this was one of the wonders of France which we simply must stop and visit. The fabulous Château of Champigny was destroyed in 1635 by Cardinal Richelieu out of jealousy, believing that such beauty nearby would detract from the splendours of what he himself was having built. But the Sainte-Chapelle, so named because it originally housed a fragment of the True Cross, was saved and remains perhaps the most beautiful Renaissance building in France.

We rode through the sleepy village of Champigny. Across a dry moat rose the Sainte-Chapelle's wonderfully elegant tall buttresses and huge pointed windows topped by a high slate roof and steeple. There is an astonishing lightness and harmony to it all with flying buttresses, pinnacles and gargoyles leaping into space. We tied the horses to a grill by the entrance, rang the bell and were admitted. There were no other visitors and we had the whole place to ourselves. We pushed open the superbly carved door into the chapel itself and both gasped at the sheer glory of it. Soaring columns in a white dream leading up to the vaulted roof, perfectly proportioned empty space surrounded by incomparable gracefulness. The once magnificent choir stalls, statues, paintings and tapestries were lost or destroyed during and since the Revolution and perhaps the perfection is enhanced by their absence. But the astonishing stained glass has miraculously survived and it is the most famous feature of the chapel. We still had quite a way to ride that day and so could not linger, but one thing struck us immediately about the windows. In several of them Louis IX (St Louis) is shown leading the Crusade. The horses on which he and his cavalry are mounted are all white. We were told in the Camargue that the fortunes of the region had fluctuated over the centuries with the demand of the French army for horses, the Camargue horses' particular qualities of endurance and courage making them ideally suited for warfare. Moreover, as we already knew, St Louis set out for both the Seventh and Eighth Crusades from Aigues-Mortes on the edge of the Camargue. It would be only logical that he would obtain horses for his cavalry locally. There was a good chance, therefore, that those shown in the stained glass were the remote ancestors of our Thibert and Tiki tied up outside. In the ninth window the battle of Massource is depicted, the white horses on the left being ridden by Arabs in turbans wielding scimitars, while those on the right, caparisoned with fleurs de lis, carry Frenchmen in armour. It is a marvellously lively picture full of waving swords and lances, fallen bodies and serried ranks of opposing foot soldiers. But as in the somewhat similar *Rout of San Romano* painted by Paolo Uccello a hundred years before the chapel was finished and the windows installed, the horses are rather wooden like rocking horses and, try as we might, we could not see any difference in characteristics between those on either side.

Herta had even made the arrangements for our next night for us. She was so kind and knew so many people that we told ourselves that if we had gone to see her before setting out she would have found friends to help us all the way across France. At Rivière, the very spot where we reached the Loire as it flowed past Chinon, we turned through the grand gate of yet another château. This time it was a delightfully decorated 19th-century folly, the façade a profusion of pretty windows. Once again we were expected and like an Advent calendar the windows popped open and shut as we trotted up the gravel drive, to reveal curious elderly ladies, maids with white collars over their black dresses, daughters and friends peeping out at us. The owner, M. le Comte de Monteynard, a round, jolly hunting man who was also the elected Mayor of Rivière, was standing on the steps to greet us, his wife in working overalls beside him. They cheerfully showed us a field for the horses and said the young were welcome to camp in the garden.

They also willingly agreed that we might film a sequence in their cellars during which the Count would tell us about the wine he produced at the château. He assured us there was plenty of electricity for this purpose down there. The BBC electrician nearly had a fit when he found that this consisted of two naked wires running along the ceiling, to which he had to clip his terminals. However, he managed to set up his lights, one of the rows of ancient barrels was tapped and we were filmed holding our glasses up to a candle, sniffing and tasting with knowledgeable and appreciative expressions on our faces. The wine, a light Chinon with a faint aroma of raspberries, tasted especially delicious in those circumstances as the Count extolled its virtues and we were happy to go through several takes in order to get it just right. In the middle of filming Michael and Serena arrived with Jamie and Alex, so that by the time we all repaired to the drawing room 'to sample some of the '64' there were a dozen of us. We had lunched on the way at an excellent workmen's café where the carafe wine had been included with the price of the meal and as we were all due to return to England the next day we had done ourselves better than wisdom would have dictated.

Everyone was in high spirits, the Monteynards were excessively generous and I could feel the situation deteriorating as the afternoon wore on. The BBC team had decided that this was the wine with which to fill their duty-free allowance and, urged on by the Count, were sampling several different vintages at once. Jamie was emptying our possessions out of the car on to the lawn, laying out the tents and trying to sort out Rupert's things for him to take to school. Rupert meanwhile was attempting to string his hammock between two ornamental trees which bent towards each other when he climbed in to test it, depositing him on the ground. Michael and Serena at least were sober and so, taking Alex with us for a last lesson in how to tack up Tiki, we slipped away to introduce the horses to their new riders.

Resisting the temptation to help, since she would be on her own tomorrow, Louella watched Alex struggle with the complicated straps and buckles which had now become second nature to the rest of us. Meanwhile I introduced Michael to the mysteries of the Camargue saddle, since he might well have to take it off during the day when Jamie was not there to help. We began to explain how very different the technique of riding these horses in these saddles was from the English hunting field where Michael and Serena were completely at home.

As they mounted for the first time we had a moment's misgiving as we saw how much bigger they both were than us and how small the horses looked underneath them. But then we reminded ourselves how burly the *gardians* in the Camargue had been and how tough Thibert and Tiki really were; and they certainly looked frisky enough as they cantered off around the field. The same could hardly be said for their riders. Camargue saddles are made individually to fit the purchaser and I had been lucky to have the same measurements as John Skeaping in that area. Michael's bottom was, however, at least two sizes larger and could only just be squeezed in. He was to be quite painfully rubbed during the next four days. Serena was not wearing a bra and had a most uncomfortable time when Tiki trotted. Like ringmasters in a circus, Louella and I stood in the centre of the field shouting out advice to two extremely proficient riders who found themselves in the nightmare situation we both remembered from our first Camargue ride, when none of the normal signals work.

'You must sit well down in the saddle!'

'Lean well back and relax. Don't try to rise in the stirrups!'

'Don't let him trot! Cantering slowly is much more comfortable.'

'Drop the reins! If you gather them up he'll go faster!'

That evening we continued to heap advice on them until it was a wonder that they did not tell us to shut up or they would go home. Fortunately the GR3 runs from Chinon all along the Loire and, being one of the major footpaths across France, we hoped it would be well marked for them so that navigation should not be a problem. Jamie was perfectly calm and confident that he could handle any eventualities. 'Go home and enjoy your days off,' he said, 'Alex and I will both look after them.' Michael and Serena made reassuring noises, too, and seemed eager to be off. We tried not to worry but were both still fussing like old hens as we helped them get ready in the morning. In their smart white breeches, shining black boots and hard hats, they looked much more professional than we had done in our check shirts and leather chaps but it was still a wrench to see them ride off towards the river without a backward glance.

11

Michael's Chapter

We set out in some trepidation from the château at La Rivière, on the banks of the Vienne, where the horses had spent Friday night. Robin and Louella concealed their anxiety well, but we were very much aware that the horses had come a long way and still had a long way to go. Moreover, Thibert had heat in his off fore ankle and Tiki had a trouble-some saddle sore which only several days' rest would heal. So the nightmare was that we would be delivering unsound horses to Robin and Louella on their return four days later. On top of that, I was a good two stone heavier than Robin and Serena about the same over Louella.

But even by the time we'd jogged into the outskirts of Chinon we were caught up in the particular quality of what we were doing. I hadn't read a map in earnest since NATO Battle Royal in 1954. I'd certainly thought of myself as quite a whizz as map-reader when commanding a troop in the 13/18th Hussars, but suddenly that seemed an awful long time ago, and Robin had made it clear that we were very much on our own. We had arranged to meet Jamie at the Royal Abbey of Fontevraud, the route seemed straightforward enough, so we might as well enjoy ourselves. Long before you get to Chinon, and long after you leave, the view is dominated by the massive presence of Richard Coeur de Lion's ruined castle on the north side of the River Vienne. Here Richard died in 1199 of a festering crossbolt wound in the shoulder sustained at the siege of Châlus, and was taken to be buried at his father's feet at Fontevraud, presumably along the path we were travelling. Certainly the bridle path led us along a very ancient route, for in the forest before Fontevraud, now owned by the French army and tragically laid to waste by tank tracks and so forth, we came upon one hundred metres or so of almost perfect Roman road, the blocks as square and the surface nearly as true as they were 2000 years ago. After only a morning in the saddle, we were getting the hang of things, and right on time jogged out of the forest to enjoy the stunning view of the Royal Abbey across the valley. I had been there three years before for an Anglo-French conference on 'Le Livre', which promised much but led to nothing, and had found the place, on which the French government has lavished huge sums on restoration, somewhat chilly. It provides an extraordinary reminder of medieval England's connections with Anjou and Aquitaine, because in the church are buried Henry II, who had been Count of Anjou, his wife Eleanor of Aquitaine, Richard Coeur de Lion, and King John's wife Isabella of Angoulême. This was one of the great abbeys of France until the Revolution, but was then converted in 1804 by Napoleon into a state jail for common criminals, which did have the merit of preserving it from complete destruction, and sparing it the fate of the monastery which became a stone quarry. It ceased to be a prison in 1963, but still holds some grim ghosts.

Jamie and Alex went on to Champigny, just short of Saumur, to find a field for the night, and we had an uneventful afternoon, marred only by losing our way, by an extraordinarily intense invasion of horseflies, and by one spectacular human saddle sore resulting from Serena's insistence, with Pony Club briskness, that she could ride Tiki bareback all afternoon and thus save *his* saddle sore. That offer wasn't repeated! But as we came into really intensive wine country we realised that Jamie would have difficulty in finding any field, let alone one fenced for horses. So, arriving before them, we went into the nearest big house to ask for help. This belonged to a captain in the French cavalry, who was a riding instructor at the school of equitation in Saumur, and while he regretted *infiniment* that he didn't have a spare stable himself he pointed us to his friends in a château down the road. The Count and Countess d'Isigny were away, but their housekeeper was most welcoming and there was a fenced paddock, hay and water. We stayed the night at the very comfortable Hôtel Anne d'Anjou under the walls of the château which overlooks the centre of Saumur, and Jamie and Alex joined us for dinner at a very solid restaurant called L'Escargot.

Sunday morning was the only unenjoyable part of our four days. A new road into Saumur from the south had made a nonsense of the map as far as the bridle paths were concerned and we had to go right into the centre of the town and then slog out through a seemingly endless suburb along the banks of the Loire, past the huge Ackermann Vineyard, which with Gratien and Meyer makes most of the sparkling wine of the district. We managed to find a parallel road away from the river, which took us onto high ground and enabled us to make good time to Gennes for lunch, but along the way we endured our one good soaking. We had booked for the night at a one-star Michelin restaurant, the Auberge Jeanne de Laval, on the north side of the river at Les Rosiers, which promised sumptuous things. But in the morning it had become clear to us that if we followed the loop of the Loire past Angers we would have no hope of covering enough ground to make our rendezvous with Robin and Louella east of Nantes on Wednesday morning. So we decided to cut across away from the river and, as it were, ride along the string rather than the arc of the bow. After lunch we made an excellent fifteen miles on a beautiful sunny afternoon trotting and occasionally cantering on the sandy cultivated soil bordering the vines which grew all along the little side roads. Jamie had landed on his feet again, finding a splendid château with some very good-looking horses in the stables, excellent paddocks, and a cross-country course in the grounds. But no one at all in sight. We took a chance, tipped the horses out into a field and left a note telling the owners who we were and where we were having dinner. They couldn't have been nicer to Jamie and Alex and were totally intrigued in the morning by our account of Robin and Louella's trip. A long Monday morning's riding, with one totally incomprehensible loss of way over which I'm still scratching my head, brought us back to the banks of the Loire at Chalonnes where Jamie had a picnic waiting at a pleasant public park on the river bank, with good grass for the horses. The heat seemed by now to have gone completely out of Thibert's leg, much to my relief, and Serena and I were really well settled into the rhythm of riding them both. Neither of us had ever ridden in these deep comfortable saddles, and we quickly appreciated the toughness and stamina of the horses, which by our normal standards were carrying a hell of a weight on their backs.

By now the bridle paths were bearing very little relation indeed to what was shown on the map, and in the afternoon we found ourselves forced more and more onto the main M751 road which runs along the south bank of the Loire from Nantes to Saumur and carries an enormous amount of heavy traffic, none of which showed any disposition to slow down for horses. On this stretch the barking dog syndrome seemed to be at its worst, with in every village and homestead a succession of Alsatians, Dobermanns, German police dogs, and plain ratty mongrels hurling themselves to the limit of their chains or against the fencing which kept them from us. The horses were far more phlegmatic about the whole business than I was, and I couldn't believe that according to the law of averages somewhere between the Camargue and Brittany one of these wretched animals wouldn't get loose and sink its teeth into one of the horses.

We were quite late, one and a half hours in fact, in linking up with Jamie at St Florent-le-Vieil, and very tired, as were the horses after so much hard work. But they had a good feed, courtesy of a very twinkly farmer from whom we bought a sack of cattle nuts (*les granules*), and we had the best, biggest, if least-heralded meal of our journey in the Host. de la Gabelle at St Florent-le-Vieil.

So far so good, with three days completed out of four, and quite a short stretch left for the last day. I was crossing every finger for the last day as we rode out of St Florent to try to find a bridle path route down beside the river. At which point an enormous Alsatian hurtled through a pair of barn doors, and across the road, seemingly straight for Thibert's throat. I screamed every imprecation I could muster, and it slammed on the brakes about a foot away from Thibert, who seemed totally unconcerned by what was happening. Serena gave the apologetic owner an earful and all was well. My faith in the law of averages was restored.

We aimed for Champtoceaux by lunch-time, and while a series of locked or wired-up gates forced us away from the footpath along the Loire we were shown a most beautiful route for the last six miles into the town, along grassy fields right beside the river with not a soul in sight and, it seemed, every bird in France singing. After lunch a very short stretch to the bridge at Mauves and everything totally straightforward. But it didn't quite work out that way. First the farmer pointed us along a lane beside the river through which, *bien sur*, we could pass. Within the space of half a mile this narrowed and narrowed, and rose and rose, until suddenly we found ourselves with a hundred-foot sheer cliff above us to our left, and the same below us to our right, and a tiny path of shale just about wide enough to take a horse. Then came a fallen tree and I had the nasty feeling of being able to go neither forward nor back. Once again, the horses were marvellous and allowed us to back them very slowly to safety. When we threaded our way back to our chosen route and trotted through fields of incredibly rich alluvial market gardens which stretch for miles to the east of Nantes and south of the river, Jamie had found probably the best grazing of all, on a lush camp site across the bridge at Mauves. It had just been closed at the end of the season, beautifully fenced, water on tap, and a very sweet old man who had had the summer licence, but not the rights for winter grazing, and so refused all offers of money. Jamie and Alex had done great detective work through the Mairie and Syndicat d'Initiative to track him down.

The hairiest moments of the journey were literally reserved for the last. The iron bridge, almost a mile long, which crosses what is by now virtually an estuary of the Loire at Mauves, is noisy and frightening enough for horses at the best of times. But creeping towards us from the far end was a moving gantry on which two men were sand-blasting rust off the sides of the bridge with fearful implements under hydraulic pressure. The noise was deafening, sand was flying in all directions, the generator added to the din, the structure was shaking, orange and white markers flapping all over the place in the wind, in short every ingredient to terrify horses out of their wits. My hunters would have taken one look at this, wheeled round and fled. But Serena got Tiki to walk straight through it, nervous certainly, but scarcely hesitating. Thibert followed on tiptoe, and we were out the other end and at the end of our journey.

Robin and Louella reading this will think we're making a hell of a fuss about just four days and perhaps 120 miles as the horses travelled, though of course much less on the map. After all it was a tiny proportion of the journey they made. But it honestly seemed epic, a wonderfully intense and satisfying time out of time, in which external time lost all meaning and our total absorption in getting from place to place, doing our best for the horses, and making our rendezvous seemed the only objectives worth considering. Jamie and Alex were great, endlessly cheerful and resourceful, and excellent company. We wouldn't have missed it for anything, it added a whole new dimension to our feeling about France, and it was London, on a humid lunch-time off the plane from Nantes, which seemed irrelevant and unreal.

12

Louella's Chapter

For my part it was difficult to leave our journey for four days, knowing all the emotion a temporary homecoming would generate. To steel yourself to eight weeks away from your children, house and responsibilities is not so difficult if everything at home is in good hands and you know they are all getting on fine without you. But suddenly to drop in on it all and then whizz off again would, I felt, be unsatisfactory and unsettling. The children would want a hundred per cent of my time, certain family and friends would have to be squeezed into an already impossible schedule, and we had the even more important task of last-minute shopping and endless name-taping to get Rupert off to a new school. So I was reluctant to leave the horses and the familiar pattern of moving on each day, alone with Robin while we explored the idyllic French countryside, talking for hours on end as many couples never have the chance to do. It was with a mixture of excitement and unwillingness that I set off to take up my other role in life of mother and housewife. It seemed rather pointless to drive from Chinon to Roscoff in a car if we were then going to fly back just to ride the same route on a horse. Also the emotional strings pulling me home to my children were fragmented by my wish to stay with Tiki. I felt we were a team that shouldn't be trespassed on, and it was with great anxiety that both Robin and I handed over our faithful friends to two strange custodians. Although Michael and Serena are better and more experienced riders than we are, we felt sure they would all come to grief without us to look after them all. How far from the truth that turned out to be.

The romance of our ride through France was very strong for us both as we had been married less than a year, and this was our first expedition together.

I have adored Robin since he and Marika, with Lucy a few months old, moved to Cornwall twenty-five years ago. They bought a moorland farm six miles from where I lived and my parents were one of the first local couples to meet them. Robin's nephews John, aged ten, and Richard, eight, were at prep school in England, flying home to Jamaica whenever possible. But on the occasions they needed a home in England, half-terms and weekends out, they lived at Maidenwell. My twin brother and I were the same age as Richard and loved going to Maidenwell to play with the boys who soon became our firm friends. When I was twelve my parents went to Hong Kong for three years and so my English haven for many a half-term and Easter holiday was Maidenwell, riding, swimming and being a constant guest. I loved it all, and I adored both Robin and Marika who were very happy and managed to infect others with their love for each other as well as everyone and everything around them.

When I was fourteen Robin wrote to my parents asking if he might name a yellow labrador puppy Louella, after me. I was very flattered, although I am afraid my canine namesake left much to be desired. Large, fat and lazy, she shamed all by her inability to retrieve anything out shooting, and her constant interest in the opposite sex. Ten years later Robin made the 'friend of the family' speech at my wedding with the panting, adoring Louella at his feet while he compared her with the bride he had known since childhood. It was a tricky topic which he managed to carry off without offending either Louella. My small page, blond, blue-eyed and six was Rupert, the much longed-for and enchanting son Robin and Marika had had ten years after Lucy had been born.

Robin truthfully claimed in his speech that he alone was responsible for teaching me to ride, waterski, type and drive, and his help with my homework over the years had got me through my 'O' levels. The only one even his patience had failed to make me pass was French. Perhaps I would have tried harder had I known seventeen years later I would wish I could speak it as we rode together, married and very much in love, through the entire length of France.

After six and a half years of marriage and two sons I found myself alone again, living in London and in the twelfth year of working for the Department of the Clerk of the House in the House of Commons. I loved my job and all the people I knew through it, and it did not occur to me to feel life was unfair or unkind. For Robin life was both; in that Marika tragically died aged forty-four of cancer, after a lengthy and very brave fight against it. She had led a life that leaves me breathless just thinking of her achievements. Her death ended a career in broadcasting and journalism, thirty-six published books on cookery, travel and children's stories that would make anyone feel inadequate. She managed to do all this as well as entertain generously, create a beautiful house and garden, bring up two children and still manage to travel with Robin to the far ends of the earth. It was these shared expeditions that made Robin realise it was not always necessary to leave his wife behind: it's a legacy I am grateful to inherit.

I firmly believe that much in life is meant and that when we come to a crossroads the decision which way to go has already been made for us. This maxim of things being 'meant' helps me to cope philosophically when things go wrong and life does not turn out the way I planned. I also know that timing is important and so I count every blessing that when I found myself alone aged thirty-one, after a very quick divorce with as little animosity as there can be in these things, I was able to view the future with excitement and a sense of strength.

I had two gorgeous sons of four and a half and just two, and a nanny they adored. I bought a flat a mile and a half from their father's house in North London and did it up with the help of a girlfriend and a Polish builder who had been a colleague of Lech Walesa. He could not return to his mother country and his wife and child in Gdansk for fear of imprisonment, and they could not leave Poland to be with him. How lucky we are that freedom is something we can take for granted. Harry and Peter and their nanny could use both my flat and their old home; their school, friends and favourite walks remained the same, while I went on with my job at the House of Commons. I am sure it helped the children to adapt gently to their new life and they did not seem to suffer, even finding it all rather fun, a little strange, perhaps, but definitely an adventure.

Robin and Marika meanwhile had time to reconcile themselves to an illness that was slowly sapping her strength and tremendous energy. This does not make it any less difficult to bear when a loved partner of twenty-four years dies but it is a little easier to be tidy about details and arrangements and to cope efficiently.

Robin was remarkably brave when Marika died; and her own strength right up until her death helped all her family considerably. He spent a few quiet weeks at home and then he and Rupert flew off to Kenya for the Christmas holidays to stay with George Adamson and to marvel at his work with the lions at Kora. Robin had been approached a year before by a much-respected French publishing house and asked to write his autobiography. The time now seemed right to tackle this project without distraction. He found it enormously therapeutic and a perfect time to record what he considered to be the first half of his life.

While all this was happening we met in London at a dinner party. We had always kept in touch throughout both our sad times but I had not seen him since Marika's memorial service. We began seeing each other, went hot-air ballooning together – a first time for both of us – and discovered it was not entirely due to the balloon that we had our heads in the clouds. Having always been best friends, it would have been almost impossible not to fall in love. Nothing about each other was not already known; he had been my childhood idol, my teenage friend and my adult companion. My being Cornish and living within a large family most of whom were Cornish-based meant my home ties were very strong, and it helped that Robin knew them all as well, if not better, than I did. I had known Robin all his married life and had watched and loved both his children from birth. Lucy was a special friend, only eight years younger than me. I had once lived at Maidenwell for ten months over Rupert's birth and been both untrained secretary to Robin and Marika, and helper and companion to Lucy. There were no fears for me that my stepchildren were an unknown or unwelcome factor. They were a bonus. I only hoped they would like the idea of me as a stepmother.

They were, of course, kind and helpful and we all adapted relatively quickly to what is never an easy role change. I can never be their mother and it is not a relationship without its problems because stepmothers are, when the chips are down, an obvious target. But Rupert realises that it is nice to have me about for a variety of useful reasons, and I know whilst Harry and Peter adore him, he is very tolerant of them and extremely kind. Lucy has married and now lives in London with a weekend cottage in Gloucestershire, but she comes home when she can.

We were married in London on a crisp November day just over a year after Marika died, with Lucy and three other friends as our witnesses and entire wedding party. Lucy and Hugh had announced their engagement in the papers that morning. The four of us went out to dinner and it made our own wedding day complete to see them both so very happy too.

The next day I was back at work in the House of Commons. However, Kenneth Bradshaw, who put up with me for about five years as his personal secretary and who had recently become the Clerk of the House, gave us a lovely lunch-time party in his flat overlooking the River Thames. All my friends throughout both Houses were there, and Mr and Mrs Speaker found the time to come and drink our health. Robin made a short speech: this time not as a friend of the family, but as my husband.

We had decided to delay having a honeymoon as I wanted to work until the end of the year – another five weeks. During this time I had one week of work in Paris with the Western European Union, and Robin and I managed to fly down to the Camargue for our second visit there, again staying with Maggie Skeaping.

1983 ended, and I said goodbye to the House of Commons and a good many friends. But the excitement of moving to Maidenwell and back to my roots was tremendous, and I was soon happily ensconced and marvelling at the beauty of a house I had never stopped to observe in detail. I have not wanted to change it, I have no ghosts to exorcise, and I was made instantly welcome as its new custodian. The garden is beautiful and we are keen to learn and expand both our knowledge of it and its size. We open it three times a year for charity and have a marvellous response, visitors sometimes from long distances coming time and time again.

In the spring we had our 'honeymoon' and went for three weeks to Jamaica and the Cayman Islands. Lucy came to stay in Jamaica with us. The three of us were generously looked after by one of Robin's brothers, Patrick, who owns a 2000-acre plantation near Falmouth, in the district of Cornwall. We swam off his private beach, ate wonderful local fish, and lay in the hot sun content to do little but laze. When Lucy flew off to New York and then back to Hugh and house-hunting, we went to stay with friends of mine in the Cayman Islands. Our own beach and beach-house, a sports car and privacy – the most understanding honeymoon hosts. We had not been really alone, ever, until those five days in Cayman.

The summer was spent idyllically at Maidenwell while plans were made for the Camargue trip, and when the day dawned to drive to France we were highly organised and ready to go.

And now here we were five weeks later, used to sleeping in a different place each night, sometimes camping sometimes not, always on the move, a daily pattern of peace and solitude. The ostrich approach to life seemed very attractive. I could have ridden on every day forever and had no wish to break our routine for four hectic days back home.

Once home, paradoxically, we had no desire to go back to France. The children were excited to see us, we had much to do, news to catch up on and things to see on the farm and in the garden. Everything had been taken care of so well that we seemed hardly to have been missed. Rupert and I tramped from one shop to another in Bodmin looking for rugger boots, track suits, grey socks and dozens of handkerchiefs, and I spent the evenings naming it all regardless of the family and friends who came to supper every evening to hear our news. We were sad to see Rupert go, but he was looking forward to his new school and friends and I think five weeks of travelling through France in the car had been enough for him. We left him at the school, looking small and rather forlorn with a trunk nearly as big as himself and an earful of unwanted advice. We went on to London and flew the next morning to Nantes to pick up our journey 200 km further on from where we had left it four days before. A quick cup of coffee in the airport cafeteria with Michael and Serena before they flew home showed us all had gone well. Jamie and Alex had proved to be just as efficient a back-up team to them as Jamie and Rupert had been to us. They had all got on well, thoroughly enjoyed their four days riding, and the horses were well and did not appear to have missed us at all.

13

The Nantes-Brest Canal

Louella and I arrived at Nantes Airport on one of the rare direct flights from London. Having heard nothing for the four days we had been away, it was a huge relief to see Michael and Serena looking bronzed and healthy beyond the glass doors as we cleared Customs. They were to fly back on the same plane and so we only had time for a quick cup of coffee as it was refuelled; but this was long enough to put our minds at rest, both that there had been no disasters and that they had had a good time.

Jamie and Alex took us to the deserted camp site on the edge of the river at Mauves-sur-Loire where they had left the horses. Everyone had got on well without us and as we gave Thibert and Tiki an extra critical examination we felt that they could have shown more overt pleasure at our return, representing as we did their beloved owners and considerably less weight than they had been carrying along the Loire. But even Camargue horses will not go that far and we had to be content with the way they hurried over to us when we called them. Tiki's saddle sore was worse and looked quite unpleasant, being over an inch across and weeping, although clean and healthy from being dressed each day. It was not sensitive to touch, however, and did not seem to bother him, so there was nothing for it but to keep it protected and carry on.

Thibert, too, was beginning to develop a couple of bare patches on his back where the saddle rubbed and it looked as if the skin would break soon. Their feet were in good shape from the regular oiling they were receiving, but Thibert had a nasty place on one of his heels, which Jamie said he thought must have come from a rope burn when his *seden* had become wrapped around it. There was a little pus and we decided to treat it with the antiseptic aerosol spray. This, of course, made him totally neurotic about having that foot touched at all, even to having the hoof picked out before setting out in the morning. When similar 'burn' marks appeared later on Tiki's feet, we realised we must have diagnosed the problem wrongly and thankfully stopped trying to spray it. We subsequently learned that it was caused by a parasite which could be simply removed by washing the feet with the correct lotion. The lameness in his off fore had happily cleared up completely.

Leaving the horses to enjoy the rest of their day off grazing the plentiful grass at the camp site, we all went in the car to recce the route ahead. We had been advised that for much of the remaining journey we would be able to ride along the Nantes–Brest canal and we were eager to see if it really was going to be as easy as it sounded. For the last 20 km or so into Nantes the canal joins the river Erdre and runs through the Lac de Mazerolles without a towpath, but thereafter we hoped to find an ideal surface with no gates or hills taking us some 250 km towards our destination. And so it proved. Our first view of the canal was at a pretty little lock at the end of a country lane. There were bright red geraniums in a bed beside the lock keeper's cottage and everything was neat and well looked after. The towpath was wide enough to drive the car along and it was even mown. Expecting some form of discouragement, we asked if the canal really went all the way to Brest.

'Bien sur,' the jolly lady weeding her garden replied.

'And may we ride along it on horses?' we enquired.

'I can see no reason why not,' she said. 'After all, people go along on bicycles and even in cars sometimes, although they are not supposed to. I am sure you will have no trouble.'

It seemed too good to be true that life should suddenly have become so easy.

Near Blain we located a promising looking field and went to see the ruins of the castle. Not much is left, but we all liked the drawbridge tower which was impressive in spite of guarding only a dry moat. It was lived in by a splendid, very old man who took us under his wing and proudly showed us his fruit and vegetable garden inside the ramparts. From here we had a fine view of the remaining 15th-century buildings, which have now been turned into a school. In return for his hospitality we bought two kilos of his nectarines from him. They were unripe and inedible but we took them back for the horses who liked them very much, sucking them noisily and then neatly spitting out the stones.

We rode up from the Loire on a perfect morning with a clear azure sky above and the whole valley below hidden in a white fog. The horses were eager to be off and stepped out well. It was very early; the smell of woodsmoke lay in the air, and invisible dogs barked in the distance as we came over the hill and saw Brittany stretching away ahead of us, green, rustic and familiar after the dry plains of central France. We suddenly began to feel that we were nearing home. The country would not change again radically between here and Cornwall.

Now there were many more cows to be passed, but both the horses had become much braver about them and hardly turned their heads if they did not rush over to us. Tiki even allowed one to lick his nose across an electric fence, although he stood poised for flight.

We saw a lot of pleasant modern houses here and it struck us that all along the way we had been regularly impressed by the architecture of even quite simple new buildings. The factories were as hideous as anywhere, but the small private houses often had unusual and attractive features which gave them great character. Here it was sometimes a slate tower neatly and cleverly designed with the slates graded from tiny at the top to large at the bottom and arranged to fan out around a dormer window. In the south there had also often been towers, but there covered in pantiles or shaped like onion domes; each different but conforming to a local style. Originality, let alone eccentricity, seems almost unknown in modern British houses.

Reaching the towpath after a morning along roads was undiluted joy. We could give the horses their heads and canter along side by side, hand in hand even, waving to passing boats. We neither had to urge them on nor hold them back: they would simply carry on until they were tired and slowed to a walk. At first five or ten minutes every hour was enough, but after a few days they were keeping going for twenty minutes or more at a stretch sometimes. All we had to do was sit back in our comfortable saddles and watch our reflections glide past on the surface of the water. There was nowhere else for them to go but ahead and almost no one else about save fishermen. When we met up with Jamie and Alex for a picnic in the middle of the day, we would unsaddle and let the horses loose to graze along the towpath. They would never go far away from us. On the contrary, the problem was to stop them walking all over us as we lay munching in the sunshine. We resolved this by leaving the car doors open as barriers to block the path. If we failed to close the windows, Tiki would put his head through to try and reach whatever had been left on the front seat. Even water was no longer a problem as all we had to do was dip our bucket in the canal.

River trips along the Nantes–Brest canal have recently become big business and on some stretches we passed a good many boats. With virtually no commercial traffic these were all tourists. When we were pretty sure they were British or American, we would call a polite 'Good morning' as we cantered past and enjoy their delayed surprise. Perhaps we deluded ourselves, but we felt that we were a dashing and unlikely sight, which may have brought some excitement into their peaceful cruising day.

Along straight stretches there were often rows of poplars, their reflec-tions marching ahead and giving a grand and formal feeling to our progress. When the canal became sinuous, looping back on itself like a meandering stream, it was still usually quicker and easier to stay on the towpath than to risk trying to cut corners along roads, as it was then easy to get lost. Also the main towpath tended to change sides so that one could rejoin the canal at a point where there was neither path nor a bridge by which to cross over.

A delightful man who had designed and built his own miniature holiday house on the canal side assured us that the local farmer would not mind the horses grazing the small field behind it. There was a deep flooded ditch to act as a barrier and he gallantly carried Louella across this on his back, leaving Jamie and me to use a vaulting pole which he had cut to the right length. He invited us to share a bottle of Gros Plant, the refreshing local Nantais wine and said Jamie and Alex were welcome to sling their hammocks between the trees beside the canal. When we drove them back there towards midnight after a good dinner, the setting looked so beautiful in the moonlight, everything silver, shimmering and still, that we genuinely regretted having decided to stay in a small hotel nearby. Early in the morning we awoke to hear rain beating on our bedroom window. Hurriedly we dressed and went to rescue the campers. They were calmly packing and quite unworried by having been soaked. It was Alex's first serious test and seeing her cheerfully wringing out her wet clothes convinced us that, as Jamie had promised, she was a more than worthy successor to Rupert. We rubbed the soaking horses down, put on our full wet-weather gear and mounted in the pouring rain. After a few hours the sun came out and in no time everything was dry again.

Between Blain and Redon the towpath deteriorated, in places being no more than a rough track through the rushes of the marshes past which the canal wandered. The earth surface had collapsed in places and often there were dangerous holes in which a horse could break a leg. We had to go slowly and sometimes make detours around fallen bridges. This stretch was much favoured by fishermen, being in places wide with deep holes where pondweed and water lilies grew. Hidden in the reeds were secret places where a crude jetty had been built or an old punt pulled ashore. These were clearly personal reserved spots, often a long walk from the nearest road but jealously guarded by their owners. Our unexpected arrival, disturbing the peace of the long afternoon, might cause one of these gentlemen to glance up from the contemplation of up to four huge rods which stretched out over the water. Sometimes our greetings were acknowledged, sometimes completely ignored. We seldom saw anything caught, though one man, who was exceptionally friendly and talkative, whether by nature or because of his success, pulled out a fat three-foot-long eel as we came on him. Smiling broadly he proceeded to cut off its head with a pair of scissors. We stopped to talk and I mentioned that we had seen several windmills but none seemed to be working. 'No,' he said. 'Now they have all folded their wings.'

One of our happiest stops was with Hervé Menager at Fégréac, a generous horseman and breeder of Welsh ponies, who showed us exceptional hospitality. His father was a local farmer and he worked as an engineer in Redon but held on to his land. After settling Thibert and Tiki in one of his better fields and insisting on giving them a generous feed of his own oats, he took us back to his house for an excellent, and unexpected cup of English tea. In the morning he rode with us for the first couple of hours and all the time we were together he talked, telling us about the history of Brittany, for which he revealed he had a great passion.

For some time I had been wondering why the very convenient canal we were following should exist at all. It must have represented a colossal amount of work, with all the locks carrying it over ranges of hills. The sea was often only 30 km or so away to the south with a series of busy ports and an expert maritime population, the coastline running more or less parallel with the canal. Why not simply carry cargo by ship between Nantes and Brest?

Hervé cleared up this problem, explaining that it was all due to Nelson. By blockading the ports and controlling the sea he had forced Napoleon to have the canal dug, largely by British prisoners of war. Ironically the cruising companies now benefiting from the boom in river holidays along it are mostly British-owned. He also told us about the great sea battle when Julius Caesar defeated the most powerful Gallic tribe in Brittany, the Veneti, in 54 BC. They were great seamen who used tall sailing ships with leather sails. The Romans were in flat barges rowed by galley slaves. They won the battle by luck and trickery, the wind dropping at the critical moment so that the oarsmen had the advantage. They then threw sickles attached to ropes into the sailors' rigging, cutting their stays and dropping masts and sails on their heads. After this all resistance in the region to the Romans crumbled and the Gauls were sold into slavery. When the Romans eventually departed some 400 years later, the country was left open to the Cornish to occupy and so become the ancestors of the present-day Bretons.

Hervé was proud of the fact that Brittany had been a largely independent kingdom for over 600 years from the time of Charlemagne until Anne of Brittany married the French King Charles VIII in 1491.

The valley on one side of which his farm lay and through which the canal ran was, for six months near the end of the Second World War, the frontier between the retreating Germans and the advancing British and American forces. As a result all houses and farm buildings on both sides of the valley, including his father's, were reduced to rubble. There were a lot of unexploded bombs in the fields and ploughing was still a dangerous business.

'That's one of the reasons,' he said with a laugh, 'why I decided to become an engineer.'

As we rode together along a series of 'green lanes' leading across country back to the canal he pointed out how there is a cross at almost every crossroad in Brittany.

'The missionaries saw to that,' he said. 'The Catholics were so shocked to find how the peasants were still following the old religion and practising secret animist Celtic rites at the beginning of the century that they made a big effort here. They had a hard time converting the people who are very stubborn about their traditions. In the far west there are beautiful stone crosses carved out of granite, but here they are mostly made of wood. When I was a child I had to cross myself each time I passed one.

'Twenty years ago the government introduced a new land tenure system to try and modernise the farming around here. The peasants objected so violently that they had to send the army in to separate those who were fighting. Even then most of the roads were still only muddy lanes like this one and outsiders had trouble finding their way around.'

In each village and hamlet we passed through there was a large communal oven where everyone baked his own bread. We also saw cider presses still in use, although as in Cornwall that is disappearing fast. However, there were apples everywhere and they were just ripening. Both the horses loved apples, although they could hardly have met them often in the Camargue, and as we rode along we would pluck them from above our heads, have a bite or two and then reach forward to pass them to our mounts. Without breaking stride they would turn their heads and take them from our hands. But when we stopped by a tree surrounded by windfalls, they were both too well trained to help themselves.

We did find the Bretons a little slower to respond to our charm than the people of central and southern France, but only marginally. We were in any case by now adept at cashing in on the strangeness of our garb and our mission so that few failed to be won over after a few minutes. The initial suspicion, nonetheless, was always there and it was fun to see it evaporate. At St Congard there was a café beside the canal and we stopped for a drink. While Louella held the horses outside, I strode in, well aware that I looked to say the least unusual in my leather chaps and black Camargue hat pushed back. The local young toughs and their girls were sprawled at a couple of tables.

'*Où sont les pistolets, alors?*' called out one to ribald laughter.

Ignoring him I went up to the bar and ordered two glasses of wine from the landlord. 'We have come a long way,' I told him loudly enough for everyone to hear.

'Oh yes, a fine Saturday *promenade à cheval*,' the wit shouted. 'Where did you hire those nags?'

'They are not hired,' I replied. 'We bought them in the Camargue and we have ridden them here on our way to England.'

Immediately the whole atmosphere changed. They were all at once on our side, wanting to know how old the horses were, how far we rode each day and wasn't it very hard, especially for Madame? It never failed. Beneath the most unlikely French exteriors we always found polite and helpful souls and their admiration was generous and unaffected. *'Quel courage!'* they cried.

Riding through towns was no longer a headache while we were following the canal as the towpath usually went right through and we hardly noticed the traffic or the people. One of the most picturesque we passed was Malestroit, full of well-preserved Gothic and Renaissance houses. One ancient slate-roofed dwelling next to the water had hideous faces carved in wood under the eaves at an ideal height for close inspection from a horse. Across the weir was a pleasant house covered in Virginia creeper, its reflection exact in the still water, with which Louella instantly fell in love. She has a thing about creeper-covered houses and, knowing this, I could usually anticipate her choices as we played the inevitable game of which of the beautiful châteaux or cottages we would really like to live in as we rode past them. We agreed that this was one of the most perfect town houses imaginable.

The next day was a Sunday and as we were making good progress we decided to let the horses have a rest while we behaved like tourists. They were grazing contentedly in a huge field next to an apple orchard from which the farmer let us feed them as many windfalls as we felt was good for them. We drove to Carnac, where only Jamie had been before as a child. There are more menhirs in Brittany than anywhere else in the world, and the greatest concentration of them is at Carnac. In spite of the houses in between and the crowds of tourists, the almost mile-long lines of standing stones are still a great spectacle. I only had to close my eyes to see columns of white-robed priests with rush tapers in their hands disappearing in procession into the pine woods to conduct solemn and dignified ceremonies. It is hard to grasp how little we know about the people who erected these colossal monuments long before recorded history.

In the afternoon we all walked barefoot along the beach at Quiberon; it was a lovely sunny day but too late in the year now for any but the most determined to be tempted into the water. Then on the way back we saw a simple hand-written sign off the main road to a *pardon* that day at Kergroix. We had heard of *pardons*, the Breton religious festivals which take place throughout the summer, but none of us had ever been to one and so we turned off. This one was too small to appear in any of the official lists and it was very much a local affair which reminded Louella and me unmistakably of our own local village carnival in Cornwall, although that has lost any religious connotations it may once have had. We had missed the procession and the church service and arrived just as the lay festival was about to begin.

The village of Kergroix consisted of little more than an earth farmyard surrounded by half a dozen houses, mostly thatched and scattered apparently at random. Only the road in was metalled, and muddy lanes and alleys between the houses led straight into the fields beyond. On an open space, a level corner of the field under the trees rather than a proper village green, trestle tables and stalls were being set up. Beside stood the tiny old church, seeming to grow out of the ground. We went inside to find a bare timbered roof and plain cemented walls. Someone had made an enchanting arrangement of mixed garden and hedgerow flowers in front of the altar. Outside we could hear the sounds of voices, snatches of song and a musical instrument being tuned, but here was a haven of perfect peace. We lit candles and sat quietly for a while. A greater contrast with the noisy tourist resort where we had lunched and the busy main road less than a kilometre away would be hard to imagine.

At first we seemed to be the only outsiders there. The locals bowed politely as we circulated, some of the women wearing the traditional costumes of black velvet embroidered dresses with lace collars and head-dresses. These are now brought out only on special occasions and are seldom seen otherwise. A young man seated at an electric organ on a platform began to play some catchy Breton music; one of the costumed ladies persuaded two men to link their little fingers with hers and dance slowly around the grassy area taking short shuffling steps. We tried our luck at some of the stalls, firing catapults at empty bottles, trying to kick a football through a suspended tyre and paying to take part in simple lucky dips. Everyone was very friendly and the stall selling home-made rough cider was doing a brisk trade.

The atmosphere of bucolic simplicity was only slightly disturbed by the arrival of a group of very mad people from the local asylum. They were accompanied by some cheerful young attendants who largely left them to their own devices, only interceding when situations began to get out of hand. We sat on the church wall as one man aged about 30 with a face which looked as though a huge weight had been dropped on it, left the others to sit down between two of the elderly costumed ladies. Another younger man, but this time exceptionally good-looking, walked determinedly around with an expression on his pale sensitive features of such intense tragedy that one felt he might burst into tears at any moment. A girl in tight purple trousers, chain-smoking with frantic nervous and extravagant gestures, talked loudly to herself without looking at anyone. The others were older and tended to hang on the arms of their attendants. When the first man started to feel the material of the old ladies' costumes and they looked terrified, one of the attendants strode over and placed a restraining hand on his shoulder. This was grabbed, placed in the man's grotesque, twisted mouth and bitten hard. At that the young nurse grabbed him by the hair and led him past the dancers back to their van. In spite of this rather extreme method of control, we could only admire the young people who were prepared to risk trouble in order to give their patients a proper outing rather than resort to the all-too-familiar easy way out of keeping them drugged, docile and indoors.

We left to search for a blacksmith as the Touffou set of shoes were now in their turn worn out. M. Roussel took some tracking down as he had moved to a riding school only a few kilometres from where our horses were lodged. As a result we were able to ride there early the next morning before his first booking. He turned out to be the best and cheapest of all. Tiki still disliked being shod and spent the whole time with his face pressed into Louella's bosom, but he was braver this time and did not need a twitch.

On we rode for three more days along increasingly beautiful and deserted towpaths. From below, the mighty walls of the castle of Josselin rising out of a sheer cliff seemed impregnable. Three perfect circular towers with pointed roofs grew straight up from the river's edge, their bases carved from the living rock. But this castle too, like so many others, had been razed by Richelieu who had the keep and five of the nine original towers demolished. He taunted the Rohan owner of the time with the words, 'I have just thrown a fine ball among your skittles, Monsieur.'

Below the château was the depot for one of the main firms hiring pleasure boats, but after this point many sections of the canal had been drained and the locks were under repair. Although this meant that we were sometimes riding alongside a muddy ditch instead of open water, it was good to see that so much effort was being made to restore the waterways of Brittany. Now beech and acacia were more common than poplar as avenues lining the canal. Carpets of beech nuts made an especially good surface for cantering and the shade of the trees was welcome in the heat of the day.

As we neared Pontivy the locks became much more frequent, sometimes rising in succession like steps as the canal passed over a steep ridge. But the gradient of the towpath was always gentle and it remained easy going for the horses. The canal turns sharply south before Pontivy where it divides, the open section continuing to the coast at Lorient.

We were able to leave the towpath here and cut across a wide wedge of open, rolling corn country. For mile after mile a straight farm track led between ploughed fields and we could canter along to be rewarded at the top of each rise with another panoramic view. Far ahead, we could see the line of poplars marking the route of the canal where it meandered through the Blovet valley towards Brest.

At Neuillac we stopped at an inn, but it seemed to be closed, although when we knocked at the door we could see someone who stepped behind a curtain and hid. Feeling hungry, we rode up to a travelling grocer's van where some housewives were buying all sorts of delicious items from the interior. We asked the jovial owner what he could let us have as a picnic and he produced sliced ham and fresh cheese but regretted that he did not sell bread with which we could make ourselves sandwiches. Immediately one of the ladies shopping told us not to move, ran into her house and returned with a long loaf and a kitchen knife. Our sandwiches were prepared for us and we bought a large bunch of green grapes to follow them. Friendship and good humour are infectious and we rode on in a state of mild euphoria in the sunshine, plucking the grapes from the bunch with our teeth and spitting the pips into the cornfield.

We rejoined the canal at a charming little manor house called Kergic-quel. It was solidly built of good grey granite, covered in ivy and with white shutters. There was a familiar Cornish feel to it. From here on the canal was still unrestored, the trees reaching out over the water to meet in the middle. Narrow and often overgrown, the lock gates hung broken on their hinges or had been shored up with concrete planks. As a result it was all even more peaceful and undisturbed than before; the lock keepers' cottages, now lived in by woodcutters or gypsies, or used as holiday homes, seemed cut off from the outside world; but the towpath was mercifully open between them and we never met a barrier we could not pass. Beyond St Aignan we joined the GR341, a well-marked footpath running alongside the Lac de Guerlédan. This artificial lake, stretching for several miles between densely forested hills, is regarded as one of the most beautiful inland spots in Brittany. We tried to follow the path and succeeded with great difficulty in leading the horses up the steep wooded slope beside the dam at the eastern end of the lake. But soon after we had to give up and make our way back to a small road as the path ran along the very crest of a stony ridge which was impassable for the horses.

That night we slept at the Abbey of Bon Repos, a romantic ruin of mostly 19th-century walls and windows. The older stable block and farmhouse had recently been converted into an excellent small hotel and there we stayed while Jamie, Alex and the horses shared a patch of grass next to the gatehouse. Our host Jean-Claude Robert had previously been an atomic scientist at Harwell, but preferred cooking delicious meals and pursuing woodcock with his Irish setter in the surrounding woods. It was a place where we might otherwise have happily lingered, but the urge to reach the Channel was now overpowering and we were off again before the sun had broken through the mist over the canal. Perhaps because we would leave it that day, the canal looked more captivating than ever. Great forests of ancient beech and oak trees lined it, their reflections dramatic in the water. Every lock cottage had a pretty flower garden to admire, fruit trees from which to snatch an apple or plum if no one was looking, often also a goat or flock of ducks.

As at almost every farm we passed in France there were rabbits in outdoor hutches. They were like the residents of apartment blocks, each confined to its own box from which it gazed without interest through the bars at the world beyond. They must contribute a major part of the French diet, yet in England practically no one keeps rabbits for eating. Next to them was always a chained-up dog to shatter the peace with a hysterical reaction to the horses. At one lock there was a fine pair of swans waiting to be fed. These were a rare sight, perhaps because the number of fishermen discarding lengths of nylon line makes it a dangerous life for swans.

We celebrated our last picnic on the canal with a special feast. Jamie, who had developed a sophisticated nose for good food shops, had found some excellent smoked ham, a fresh melon cut into four thick wedges, a coarse home-made pâté, a strong Camembert and, his specialité, an outstanding *tarte aux pommes*. We came round a bend in the canal to find that Alex had laid it all out on a grassy bank under a spreading tree so that it looked irresistibly appetising. The horses joined us, finishing off the last of the nectarines and biting off the ends of the long French loaves for which they had developed a quite unhealthy taste. Tiki even leaned over Louella's shoulder and took another bite just as she was preparing to spread butter on her half. We tended to lay off the wine at mid-day, partly to keep Jamie sober for the afternoon's driving and partly because we more than made up for our abstension in the evenings. Instead, Jamie and I drank *panachée*, the French bottled shandy; the girls preferred lemonade and the horses had canal water.

Soon afterwards, we said goodbye to the canal and headed due north towards the Arrée Mountains lying between us and the coast.

14
The Channel and Home

To wake up and see a new church steeple outside our bedroom window each morning, silhouetted against a clear blue sky, was good. Usually villages were quiet in the early hours with only a few cocks crowing in the distance and the chiming of the church clock to mark off the hours. To lie for a few more moments knowing that we would be spending the whole day riding through the French countryside or along a canal with nothing else to worry about, was wonderful. On the morning of our last full day's ride in France we heard cheerful whistling for the first time. A Breton farmer setting out to work was merrily and unselfconsciously accompanying himself with a loud and tuneful melody and it struck us that this was unusual. Although we had found that people in the French countryside were unfailingly kind and generous once the ice was broken, we had also noticed that they seemed much more reserved than their counterparts in England, or indeed elsewhere in Europe, where it is quite normal to call out a greeting to a friend or stranger met on the road. Not only did the French tend not to do this, or only to return our greetings after a fractional hesitation, but those who did not know they had been observed would often step out of sight. Time and again we glimpsed a figure as we passed a village house or country farm furtively moving back behind a curtain or open doorway. We speculated as to whether this was just the innate shyness of a peasant population or whether it might have something to do with their land having been occupied by foreign invaders twice within living memory. Most tourists to France have noticed how the initial reaction to strangers there is more reserved than elsewhere. We had found that off the beaten track the contrast was even more striking.

We all stayed for our last night on the road at the Auberge de la Truite, a famous inn near Huelgoat, where the restaurant had been awarded a Michelin star. We feasted on *cailles aux bigarreaux*, drank too much wine and stuffed ourselves on wonderful sticky puddings. At last we could tell everyone that we had as good as made it: we had ridden right across France. It was all too much for Jamie, who passed out on his way through the kitchen, keeling over to bring a pile of utensils down with a crash. Mme Le Guillou, the ancient proprietress, was most understanding when he recovered and apologised, saying it was only to be expected after all the excitement of our adventure. She showed us around her fine collection of decorated box beds, carved wardrobes and linen chests, which she had rescued from her extensive family as they gave them up and changed to modern furniture. Holding a large magnifying glass in front of her failing eyes, she pointed out the carved heart and bird motifs and bewailed the lack of craftsmanship around today.

Close by was an establishment which hired out horse-drawn caravans and for a time we were able to follow an abandoned railway line which now served as one of the routes for tourists travelling in this way. It led us through some of the wild and unspoilt countryside of the Armorique Regional Nature Park which now encloses the whole area of the Arrée mountains. We followed a tumbling stream through romantic wooded hills before coming out on the desolate uplands below the jagged peaks of the Trévézal Rock, the highest point in Brittany. Although it only reaches a maximum of 384 metres, which hardly qualifies it to be called a mountain, it did make a dramatic and striking silhouette against the clouds scudding in off the Atlantic. Our own Brown Willy, the highest 'mountain' in Cornwall, which rises behind Maidenwell, our farm, is slightly higher at 425 metres and the moorland on to which we emerged felt very like home for a time. Then we were over the ridge and could see the glint of the sea far ahead. Between lay an even more familiar landscape of white houses and scattered villages across which alternate patches of brilliant coastal sunlight and cloud shadow passed. It could have been North Cornwall, looking down from Bodmin Moor towards Wadebridge and Rock, except that the churches had tall steeples instead of squat towers. Against the sea we could just make out the wonderfully tall and thin belfry of the Kreisker Chapel in St Pol-de-Léon to which we were headed.

For once the horses showed that they were tired and they needed constant urging to prevent them slouching along with heads hanging. We were tense with anticipation so that time dragged and our progress seemed painfully slow. We had finally left the last of the footpaths and were following country lanes across intensively cultivated farmland. Late in the afternoon we reached Taulé, our final rendezvous, and dismounted thankfully to sit on the church steps and wait for Jamie and Alex to turn up. Schoolchildren poured out of the schoolhouse across the square and crowded around the horses. They were thrilled by our story and one little girl rushed off with one of our fliers to tell the teacher. I overheard two small boys discussing Tiki's sex.

'C'est une jumelle,' said one firmly.

'Non!' announced the other, bending down to peer underneath. *'Regards! Il a un zizi comme nous. C'est un cheval!'*

Jamie arrived crestfallen at having failed to find a field in spite of trying all day. As this looked the most promising direction, we rode and drove in convoy along the main road back towards Morlaix, stopping at each farm gateway to ask if they had a field where we might leave the horses. At one we were told regretfully that they had no grass, at the next that the land did not belong to them. The third place we tried was called Le Hun, where we were greeted by M. Joseph Kerbrat, who had just finished milking his 17 cows and was driving them across the road with his small grandson. I explained our needs and he asked if our horses would respect an electric fence. When I assured him that they would, he said to wait until he had finished putting the cows in *their* field, when he would look after us. He took us to a perfect field with water and not too much grass. I explained that we now had four days to wait before the ferry, on which we were booked, sailed across to Plymouth. Would it be possible for the horses to stay in his field that long? We would of course pay him a fair rent for it.

'It will be a privilege to serve you after such an arduous journey,' he replied, 'and there will be no question of payment.'

We had noticed that to his grandson he spoke Breton, still very much a living language in the west of the region. Perhaps it was this, combined with the suitably shabby clothes he was wearing for milking his cows, that led me to underestimate M. Kerbrat's intellect, though not his charm and generosity. When, a couple of days later, I gave him a French copy of my autobiography, I apologised that he might find some of the chapters on my life among the Indians of South America of little interest. I was astonished and not a little ashamed when he replied, 'Not at all. I am very much looking forward to reading it as I enjoy finding out about other cultures and have several books by leading French ethnologists beside my bed at present. I have also recently become very concerned about the destruction of the tropical rain forest.' Unlike far too many people in Britain, the French do still read books.

When we eventually left and I again insisted that he accept at least 100 francs for the horses' keep, he said, 'No. I would prefer you to give the money to your charity Survival International.* I have been reading your book and would like to help the Indians.'

Having no idea where we would stay that night, we drove on the spur of the moment to St Pol-de-Léon, simply because it looked so lovely in the evening light. Once there, where else could we stay but the Cheval Blanc, happily the best hotel in town. Jamie and Alex set up the tent at

* I am President of Survival International, the organisation which defends the rights of tribal peoples.

a camp site on the beach. Behind them lay the open sea sprinkled with rocky islets; beyond lay England.

Since we would not be allowed to take the horses on the ferry unless they were boxed, we had brought a horse trailer with us on our way out and left it at Roscoff. We collected this from the shipping agents and thus were able, when the BBC team arrived, to transport the horses to wherever they wanted to film us. First we all drove back to the Nantes–Brest canal. There we were able to canter along on one side while David Saunders, the cameraman, was driven along the other, our reflections keeping pace in the water between us. We picnicked yet again and on cue Tiki performed for the camera, walking up and accepting a proffered French loaf. It seemed as though these would be the most evocative and magical scenes that could be taken to capture the long happy days when we had ridden alone together. But they were to be surpassed the next day. In Roscoff we rode through the streets while the mayor himself arranged our reception at different locations. First Louella entered the boulangerie to buy some bread and pastries for us to take home. Tiki followed her into the shop to the distress of the regular patrons and the delight of Howard, who had set up the cameraman and lights inside in the hope that just this might happen.

Outside, in the Rue des Johnnies, there just happened to be the best known onion 'johnnie' of them all, Jean-Marie Peron, who told us as he transferred strings of onions, garlic and shallots from his bicycle to the pommels of our saddles that he had been going to Edinburgh ever since 1923. Then, aged 11, he had walked all the way.

Finally, we rode down on to the beach below one of the seawater clinics where people come to be cured by the almost miraculous waters of the bay. The mayor told us proudly that there are only two places in the world with waters as pure and as clear as that at Roscoff – and they are in California and Japan. Even racehorse owners, including the film star Alain Delon, bring their horses here to walk in the sea between races to cure any lameness or sores they may have. Where better to clean and refresh Thibert and Tiki after all they had been through? Between torrential showers and periods of brilliant sunshine, we galloped back and forth across the beach, now heading out into several feet of water, now racing across the sand. In spite of being soaked, the horses loved it, and we could almost feel the salt water doing us all good. David said it was the best bit of film he had taken all year.

One of the first things we had noticed about the horses after we took delivery of them in the Camargue had been the peculiar flies which came with them. They reminded me at first of the nasty yellow flies which I remembered infesting camels in the Sahara, crawling all over their bodies. These were smaller and blacker, but there was something equally sinister about the way they scuttled for cover, hiding in folds and crevices around the horses' rear ends. When grooming we would flick dozens away from under their tails and between their legs, but they simply flew off to return and land somewhere else. They were almost impossible to kill with a blow; the hardest direct hit with the flat of the hand had no effect at all. We called them 'Armour-plated bum flies' and learned to ignore them. As we had travelled north in the late summer and the nights became colder, we had noticed that their numbers had become greatly reduced. Less than a dozen could be found on each horse by careful inspection and these seemed to be huddling together for warmth. One night in the Cheval Blanc, Louella found one on her body while she was taking a shower and saw that it had bitten her. She flicked it into the bath and battered it with her shoe before flushing it down the plug hole. When she went back into the bathroom after dinner she found that it had crawled back up into the bath and was grimly climbing up the side. It took another series of direct hits to dispose of it finally. Worried that we might be importing a new pest into Britain, which might proliferate and cause all sorts of problems, we thought the time had now come to get rid of them finally. On veterinary advice we obtained a lotion with which we washed the horses' backsides and tummies, soaking the flies before they could escape. The next day there were none to be found.

I later made enquiries among scientist friends and learned that these flies, called Hippobosca sp. equina, do exist in England, being found on New Forest ponies. They are parasitic blood-suckers similar to Tsetse flies, which transmit sleeping sickness, but these ones appear to do no harm. We at least were glad to be rid of them, even though Thibert and Tiki did not seem to notice.

On our last afternoon together Jamie, Alex, Louella and I went for a long and bracing walk around the headland behind Carantec. The wind was blowing straight in off the sea and we could barely stand against it. The thousand rocky islands of the Bay of Morlaix were drenched in white spray, alternately lit by the dazzling, pristine clear sunlight of Brittany and swept by torrential squalls of rain. There was a sense of end-of-term hysteria in the air; we had succeeded in what we set out to do without disasters, accidents or even a row. We raced each other over the sand and over the rocks, taking silly photographs and running to shelter from the rain. It was sad that we were about to split up and go our separate ways, but we could do so with a sense of achievement. Alex had been excellent company and without Jamie's constant cheerfulness and calm efficiency the whole journey would have been much less fun.

That evening at the ferry port Thibert and Tiki were inspected by a splendid black-bearded local vet, who took a shine to the horses and was extremely efficient and businesslike. He said that they were in remarkably good health and certified that they did not have any infectious diseases. We did all the paper work, loaded the horses into their trailer and waited for the ship to arrive from Plymouth. When it came in, late after a very rough crossing, the Captain said that there was no way he would take horses across in a Force 9 gale and we would have to wait until the next night. The BBC would wait with us, but Jamie's term at Aberdeen University was about to begin and so he and Alex braved the storm – and wrote later to tell us that it had been one of the worst crossings any of the crew could remember. We took Thibert and Tiki back to their field in the horsebox.

The BBC team were to spend the extra day filming another assignment in Brittany. Louella and I were free to do what we wanted. We spent the morning with the horses, grooming them especially well, treating their minor ailments and cleaning all our tack. Then we drove back to the Arrée Mountains, stopping to look at the amazing calvary at St Thégonnec on the way. We climbed to the top of the Trévézal Rock and sat in the shelter of a boulder looking out over one of the finest views in all of France. It was clear enough to see the Mont St Michel just showing above a sea haze far to the north-east. The north coast was spread out like a map below us while to the south-west we could see all the way to the estuary of the Loire, back over the route we had ridden. Like the day seven weeks before when we had looked out from Les Baux across the route ahead it all seemed a very long way, but now it lay behind us. There is something very special about seeing a country from a horse rather than from a car or bicycle, or even on foot. The freedom riding gives the traveller to observe the passing countryside and feel a part of it; the freedom to detour over almost any terrain, to go fast or slow across country, up or down hill; the need to be, to some extent, a part of every rural community visited, because the horses will need grass, fodder and water, blacksmiths and saddlers; the opportunity to talk to country people about matters which are often also their daily preoccupations; all these conspire to make the rider feel less of an interloper than any other type of traveller. As we lay in the heather and looked back across the largest state in Europe across which we had just ridden, we were able to tell ourselves that we had probably given almost as much pleasure as we had received. Time and again, children had run out of their houses to point and shout, *'Maman, regards les jolis chevaux!'* When we had waved, as we had always made a point of doing, however glum or preoccupied we might have been feeling at that moment, housewives sitting in their windows, old men in gardens, farmers in their fields, workmen on building sites, all had smiled and waved back. As a result France would never be the same again for us. The brittle exterior with which the French seem to protect themselves from foreigners would no longer be able to conceal the soft centre which we had learned lay behind.

During the day the wind dropped and by evening the sea was almost calm again. This time we were allowed to drive the horses on board. Thibert broke out in a sweat from the deafening bangs and crashes as the decks were raised and lowered and he refused to touch the water which I fetched him in a bucket from the crew's quarters. Tiki drank deep and munched quietly at the bale of hay which M. Kerbrat had insisted we take with us for them to eat during the crossing. We visited them regularly during the night, squeezing between the giant lorries bringing loads of artichokes and apples. The swell did not seem to trouble them and they wolfed down the lumps of sugar which we stole from the cafeteria.

Everything went smoothly in Plymouth when we docked at six a.m. Rosa, my secretary, who had been in charge of all the paperwork, was there to see that there were no hitches. So too was my farm partner Pancho, who would drive the car and horse trailer back while we rode the remaining 33 miles home. Beneath the cranes and gantries of Plymouth Docks, on a scruffy piece of wasteland where plastic bags blew in the wind and with the Brittany Ferries ship in the background the BBC filmed as Thibert backed out of the box and gingerly placed the first Camargue hoof on British soil.

Riding through Plymouth was strange. Paradoxically, having arrived back in our own country we felt foreign. The early morning commuters we waved to seemed to think we were mad and the schoolchildren either ignored us or whooped and made cowboy noises, assuming we were from the circus. As we crossed Union Street, Plymouth's red light district, Louella attracted the first wolf whistle since leaving the Camargue. A sentry outside a naval barracks stared straight ahead without blinking as we rode within inches of his toes and a municipal cleaner shouted at us as we rode across a grassy open space.

We stood side by side in the queue for the Torpoint ferry, moving forward with the cars waiting to board. Beside the ramp was a notice saying 'Keep clear of chain and beware of slippery surfaces. Motor-cycles, scooters and cycles, etc., must wait here until told to proceed.'

We joined a group of schoolchildren with pushbikes and were called on last by an impassive attendant who waved us to a gap between two cars, as though horses crossed on the ferry all the time. The ramp was metal, noisy and slippery. Thibert did not want to go up it and had to be given a lead by Tiki. The BBC were filming all this and it was, of course, raining. We dismounted and stayed rather self-consciously holding the horses surrounded by schoolchildren holding their bicycles.

One of the boys came over and asked where they were from and I told him 'The Camargue'. 'I thought so,' he said. 'We spent a holiday there two weeks ago and I went for a ride on one.' I told him we had ridden them all the way back. 'Cor! You must have sore bums!' he exclaimed and went off to tell his friends. We began to feel more cheerful. When we posed for the cameras beside the sign on the far shore which said 'Cornwall/Kernow' we really began to feel that we were home.

The next eight hours as we jogged soggily through high-banked Cornish lanes passed like a dream. We took coffee off some friends en route, including Howard's family, whom we had not met before. We noticed that there were many more horses in Cornwall than in France, and Thibert and Tiki called out excitedly to each one we passed, as though telling them where they came from. We met a neighbour of ours driving his large flock of sheep towards us down a narrow lane and the horses stood rigid with alarm as they flowed by on either side and between them. We reached the local village school where Louella's two small sons Harry and Peter, who had been warned that we were on the way but could still hardly believe it when we rode up, rushed out to greet us. Both were swung up on to our saddles to give us welcoming hugs. A few more miles and we clattered down into the courtyard at Maidenwell. A banner had been strung between the gates saying 'Welcome home Thibert and Tiki'. We rubbed them down and took them to their field across the garden, where they rolled contentedly and took no special interest in their future home, preferring to get stuck into the good Cornish grass.

Next morning when we went to take them a carrot each and see how they were, they came over to the gate, quite ready to be saddled up again for another day's ride.

When, after a week's complete rest, we paid them our daily visit we thought they seemed restless. Thibert looked worried and Tiki appeared to be trying to tell us something. We realised that they felt it was high time we were all moving on. They were quite rested now and ready to carry on the journey which had become second nature. During the following winter they grew thick coats and settled down completely, learning to help round up our cattle and sheep and to make the most of the quiet times in between. But the seed of an idea had been sown and we began to plan another journey on which we might once again ride together across another country.

Appendix I

Départements Visited En Route

Bouches-du-Rhône
Gard
Hérault
Aveyron
Lot
Dordogne
Corrège
Haute-Vienne
Charente
Vienne
Indre-et-Loire
Maine-et-Loire
Loire Atlantique
Morbihan
Côtes-du-Nord
Finistère

Appendix II

Chronology of the Journey

Date	Day No.	The Route	Time
Date	*Day No.*	*The Route*	*Time*
August			
10	1	Mas de Pioch – St Laurent d'Aigouze	7 hours
11	2	Bull-running at Le Cailar	4 hours
12	3	Rest	
13	4	Montarnaud – St Guilhem-le-Désert	7 hours
14	5	Le Cros	8 hours
15	6	Near Millau	7 hours
16	7	Salles-Curan	9 hours
17	8	Rodez	8 hours
18	9	Pont Neuf (near Belcastel)	9 hours
19	10	Villeneuve	9 hours
20	11	Rest	
21	12	Marcilhac	9 hours
22	13	Near Gramat	5 hours
23	14	Lacave	6 hours
24	15	Rest – Birds & Cave	
25	16	Rest – Ballooning	
26	17	Souzet (M. Vergnes)	6 hours
27	18	Terrasson (M. Mallet)	5 hours
28	19	Payrac	7 hours
29	20	Montbrun	10 hours
30	21	St Germain-de-Confolens	10 hours
31	22	Lussac	8 hours

Date	Day No.	The Route	Time
SEPTEMBER			
1	23	Near Chauvigny	4 hours
2	24	Touffou	2 hours
3	25	Rest	
4	26	Rest	
5	27	Rest	
6	28	Richelieu (M. Bruno de Croutte)	9 hours
7	29	Rivière (Comte de Monteynard)	3 hours
8	30	Michael & Serena (Souzay Champigny)	6 hours
9	31	Michael & Serena (near Beaulieu-sur-Lyon)	6 hours
10	32	Michael & Serena (St Florent-le-Vieil)	6 hours
11	33	Michael & Serena (Mauves-sur-Loire)	6 hours
12	34	Rest	
13	35	Le Chevallerais	7 hours
14	36	Fégréac, near Redon (M. Hervé Menager)	7 hours
15	37	La Chappelle	8 hours
16	38	Rest	
17	39	St Samson, near Loudéac	8 hours
18	40	Abbaye de Bon Repos (M. Jean-Claude Robert)	7 hours
19	41	Locmaria-Berrien	10 hours
20	42	Taulé, near Morlaix (M. Kerbrat)	7 hours
21	43	Rest	
22	44	Rest – Canal Filming	2 hours
23	45	Roscoff Filming	5 hours (beach)
24	46	False Departure	
25	47	Crossing	
26	48	To Maidenwell	9 hours

Appendix III

The Camargue Horse: Its Characteristics

The Camargue horse is a hardy saddle-horse.

The large head is generally rather square and 'well attached'.

The forehead is flat, the nose straight and the lower part of the nose underdeveloped, which gives the impression of a Roman nose.

The ears are short and widely spread, and have broad bases.

The eye is flush with the head since the orbit does not stand out.

The cheek is heavy.

The mane is often very thick and long.

The coat is well-developed.

When adult, the coat colour is white, sometimes flecked with brown.

The chest is deep, the shoulder is straight and short.

The neck is short.

The limbs are strong and well formed.

The hoofs' bases are broad, and the animals are sure-footed.

The knee is large; the horse is well-jointed.

The back is short.

The haunches are strong and well-muscled.

The croup is short, well filled, and slightly sloping.

The tail, well attached, is low.

The shoulder height is about 1.35–1.45m (13.2–14.2 hands).

The weight varies between 300 and 400 kg.*

The Camargue horse frequently completes its growth only between 5 and 7 years of age.

It conserves its energy for action – this is why, at rest, it often appears relaxed and sleepy.

Sensible, lively, agile, brave, and with great stamina, the Camargue horse can withstand long fasts, endure bad weather and complete long journeys.

* This is certainly an underestimate: see Chapter 4.
† Extract translated from the 'Arrêté relatif à la race du cheval Camargue', Ministry of Agriculture, 17 March 1978.

Notes on the Camargue Horse

The terrain where the herds of Camargue horses live is marginal land suitable only for extensive grazing.

Due to this severe way of life the Camargue horse has adapted to the poor food and the extremes of weather, as it never knows a stable.

Mating takes place in total freedom without any interference from the breeder, save for the selection of the stallion.

The method used to be criticised but the success rate (of about 75 per cent) proves that this is the only way of achieving a maximum number of births. These extend from April to July without any assistance.

The foals are born black or dark grey, often with a blaze. Up to six months old they follow their mothers wherever they go. At this age they begin to lose their foal coat to become gradually pale grey (or 'white') at 5 to 7 years old.

On weaning, at about six months old, the foal is caught and marked with a hot brand on the left hip with the mark of its owner and the foal's identification number.

At about three years old the foal will learn to be lunged. First of all a sack is placed on his back, then a tight girth, then a light saddle, the stirrups of which will strike his sides.

When he ceases to react a bridle is slipped on, a bit, a cavesson and a Camargue saddle. Held by a rider, he must now follow another horse.

He will be led over soft or ploughed land (so as to tire him out). At last the horseman will mount his new horse quickly and lightly as possible.

Sometimes, especially if the first part of the breaking has been very carefully executed, all will go well. But often the reaction is violent.

It is then necessary to start again next day, taking care not to end the training session with a failure. It is during the daily practice that the young horse is licked into shape and becomes a 'made horse'.

The Camargue horse is the indispensable tool of the rancher and the *gardian* for watching over and working with the herds of bulls.

Very intelligent, performing admirably the tasks assigned to him, his incredible hardiness and his capacity to endure long rides mean that he is much sought after by equestrian tourists and long-distance riders.

His great aptitude for all sorts of training makes him a good horse for working in harness and for outdoor activities.

Index

Robin and Louella, Thibert and Tiki, Rupert, Jamie Macpherson and his girl-friend Alex Grant have not been indexed as they appear throughout the book.

Abbey of Bon Repos, 116
Aberdeen University, 5, 73
abrivado, 25, 29
Ackermann Vineyard, 98
Adamson, George, 104
agriculture, 46, 55, 56, 74, 75, 112
Aigues-Mortes, 23, 24
Aïr mountains, 62
Alpes Maritimes, 14
Alzou river, 59, 61, 64
Amazonia, 65
Angers, 98
Aniane, 35, 38
Anjou, 98
ANTE, 51
Aquitaine, 46, 55, 56, 74, 75, 112
Argentine, the, 10, 33
Armorique Regional National Park, 119
Arrée mountains, 117, 119, 123
ARTE, 116
Auberge de la Truite, 118
Auberge Jeanne de Laval, 98
Australia, 10
Auvézère river, 73
Aveyron, 46, 49, 50

Baghdad, 2
Banque Populaire, 47
BBC, 5, 21, 25, 28, 34, 44, 56–67 (*passim*), 77, 81, 84–95 (*passim*), 121–5
Belcastel (Aveyron), 51
Belcastel (Dordogne), 61, 66
blacksmiths, 16, 57, 88, 115
Blain, 108, 110
Blovet valley, 116
Bodmin, 106
Bodmin Moor, 1, 44, 119
Bonneuil-Matours, 88, 90
Boorman, John, 65
Borneo, 64
boule, 23
Brazil, 65

Brest, 108, 111, 116
bridlepaths, 3, 97, 98
Brittany, 4, 108–24 (*passim*)
Brittany Ferries, 124
Brown Willy (mountain), 119
Buenos Aires, 33
bullfighting, 25, 29

Cahors, 57
Cajarc, 56
California, 121
Camargue birds, 13, 14
Camargue horses, 1–9, 17–20, 27, 47, 50, 59, 81, 94, 113, 125
Camargue landscape, 1, 11, 13, 21, 22
Camargue saddles, 8–10, 95, 96
Carajas dam, 65
Carantec, 122
Caribbean, the, 33
Carnac, 113
castration, 7
Causses, 44, 55, 56, 57, 61
caves, 62–4
Célé, 56
Cevennes, 16, 39
Chad, 62
Chalonnes, 99
Châlus, 77, 97
Chambord, M. & Mme, 60, 67
Champigny-sur-Vende, 93
Champtoceaux, 100
Channel, The (English), 3, 117, 123–4
Charlemagne, 111
Château de Hautefort, 72
Château de Montbrun, 76, 77
Château de Rochebrune, 78
Château de Touffou, 77, 90
Château La Forge, 73
Château La Treyne, 68
Chauvigny, 81, 86
Chinese Turkestan, 20
Chinon, 77, 94–7, 102

Cirencester (Royal Agricultural College), 2
Clamel, Jean-Pierre, 27
Claret de la Touche, Comte Bernard, 85
Claret de la Touche, Guy, 85, 90, 91
Claret de la Touche, Isabelle, 85, 91
Claret de la Touche, Minouche, 85, 90, 91
Code Napoléon, 56
Common Market, 55
Confolens, 77
Cornwall, 1, 2, 7, 21, 37, 45, 74, 102–6
    (*passim*), 108, 119, 125
Cougnac, 63, 66
Crewe, Quentin, 3
Crin Blanc, 1, 2
Croutte, Bruno de, 92, 93

Daniel, blacksmith, 16, 57
Davies, Serena, 93–101 (*passim*)
Delon, Alain, 121
Devon, 48
Didcot, 50
Dijon, 26
dogs, 75, 76, 99, 100
Dordogne, 61, 67, 68, 69, 74
Duncan, Patrick, 18, 19

eagles, 64–6
Edinburgh, 121
Edwards, Harry, 14, 104, 105, 125
Edwards, Peter, 9, 21, 104, 105, 125
Emery, Alain, 2
Erdre river, 108
l'Escargot restaurant, 98
Espédaillac, 57

Fairyhouse, 2
Falmouth, Jamaica, 106
Fauvet, Anne, 24, 25
Fauvet, Frank, 24, 25, 29, 32
Fégréac, 111
Fettes, 5
Figéac, 16
fishing, 110
Fontevraud, Royal Abbey of, 97
footpaths, 3, 51
Forêt d'Etagnac, 78
French attitude to travellers, 48, 112, 113,
    123
French drivers,12, 24, 26
French food and inns, 43, 52, 70
French television (FR3), 21, 57

gardians, 2, 3, 6, 25–9, 96
Gauls, 111
Gennes, 98
Germany, 3
Gourdon, 62

gourme (strangles), 15, 16, 67, 88
Gramat, 57, 58
Grande Randonnée, Sentiers de (GR), 4,
    45, 48, 49, 51, 116
Grau-du-Roi, Le, 16

Hanbury-Tenison, Lucy, 103–6
Hanbury-Tenison, Marika, 2, 37, 102–5
Hanbury-Tenison, Patrick, 106
Hardy, Liz, 10
Harwell, 117
Hemming, John, 62
Hérault river, 35
Hermitage de Notre Dame de Belle Grace,
    40
Hoffmann, Luc, 17, 18
Hong Kong, 103
Host. de la Gabelle, 99
hot air balloons (*Montgolfiers*), 53, 66–7, 104
Hôtel Anne d'Anjou, 98
Hôtel du Barrage, 79
Hôtel Le Faisan, 92
Hôtel Pont de l'Ouysse, 60
House of Commons, 103–5
Huelgoat, 118
hunting horns, 87

Ireland, 2, 78, 79
d'Isigny, Count and Countess, 98
l'Isle Jourdain, 79
l'Isle river, 76

Jamaica, 69, 106
Japan, 121
Josselin, 115
Julius Caesar, 111
Jumilhac-le-Grand, 76
juniper berries for gin, 61

Kendall, Fabien, 65
Kent, 76
Kenya, 104
Kerbrat, Joseph, 120, 124
Kergicquel manor house, 116
Kergroix, 114
King's College, Taunton, 72
Kir, Canon Félix, 83
Knights Templar, 43

La Cavalerie, 43, 44
Lacave, 61
Lac de Guerlédan, 116
La Dormac, 70
Lamorisse, Albert, 2
Languedoc, 54
Lascaux, 19, 62, 63
La Valade, 70

Le Cailar, 25, 27
Le Caylar, 42
Leeds Castle, 76
Le Guillon, Mme, 119
Les Baux, 16, 123
Les Planques, 50
Les Rosiers, 98
Limousin, 54
logistics, 4
Loire river, 93–108 (*passim*), 123
London, 57, 101, 104–7
Lot, 54, 56, 63

MacGregor, Sue, 44, 57
Madagascar, 18
Maidenwell, 103, 105, 106, 119, 125
Maître-randonneurs, 54
Malestroit, 113
Mallet, Roger, 54, 70, 72
Marcilhac, 56, 57
Marseilles, 16
Mas de Pioch, 8, 21
Masefield, John, 58
Massif Central, 44
Massource, battle of, 94
Mauves-sur-Loire, 100, 107
Mazerolles, Lac de, 108
Mediterranean, 9
Meffre, Fernand, saddle maker, 10
Menager, Hervé, 111–12
Middle East, 2, 3
Midi, Canal du, 24
Millau, 44, 45
Mison, Jean, saddle maker, 10
missionaries, 112
Mitterand, President, 10
Moore, Dan, 2
Montarnau, 32, 34
Monteynard, Comte de, 94, 95
Montpellier, 22, 32, 39
Mont St Michel, 123
Morlaix, 120, 122

Nantes, 93, 99–101, 108, 111
Nantes–Brest Canal, 108–21 (*passim*)
Napoleon, 98, 111
Nayrolle, Paul, 16, 32, 34, 35, 57
Nelson, 111
New Forest ponies, 122
New Jersey, 69
New York, 106
Neuillac, 116
Niger, 62
North Africa, 9
Nottingham, 69

Ogilvy, David and Herta, 77–94 (*passim*)

Ouisse river, 61

Padgham, Hugh, 105, 106
pardons, 113–15
Paris, 51, 105
Payzac, 73, 74
Peccais, Canal de, 22
Perigord, 16, 69
Perkins, John, 14–44 (*passim*)
Perks, Howard, 5, 21, 28, 56, 57, 61, 67, 88, 121, 125
Peron, Jean-Marie (onion 'johnny'), 121
Persia, 2
pinède, the, 17
Pinsac, 68
Plymouth, 21, 124
Poitou, 88
Pont-de-Salars, 47, 48
Pontivy, 115
Portugal, 10
promenades à cheval, 6, 8, 17
Provence, 3, 45
Purser, Philip, 17, 23

quarantine, 3
Queaux, 80
Quiberon, 113

rabbits, 117
rabies, 3
Reagan, President, 10
Red Balloon, The, film, 2
Redon, 110, 111
Rhône and Petit Rhône, 1, 8, 13, 16, 20, 22
Ribereau, M., 83
Richard Coeur de Lion, 77, 97, 98
Richelieu, 91, 115
Rivière, 94, 97
Robert, Jean-Claude, 117
Rocamadour, 34, 56, 59–66
Rochechouart, 77
Rock, 119
Rodez, 49
Rohan, 115
Romans, 111
Rome, 20
Roque, M. ('*l'Homme à Cheval*'), 16
Roscoff, 33, 102, 121
Roussel, M., blacksmith, 115
Royal Cornwall Show, 11

Sahara, 63, 64, 121
St Aignan, 116
St Congard, 112
St Florent-le-Vieil, 99, 100
St Guilhem-le-Désert, 36–7
St Laurent d'Aigouze, 27

Saintes Maries-de-la-Mer, Les, 8, 16, 17
St Pol-de-Léon, 119, 120
Ste Radegonde, 49
St Thegonnec, 123
Salles-Curan, 45, 46
Sarlat-la-Canéda, 69
Saumur, 98, 99
Saunders, David, 121
Segonzac, 73
shooting, 78, 92
sirocco, 9
Sissons, Michael, 93–101 (passim)
Skeaping, John, 3, 5, 7, 9, 10
Skeaping, Maggie, 3, 5, 6, 7, 9, 10, 24, 29,
    105
Souillac, 68
Souzay Champigny, 98
Souzet, 69
Spain, 33
Stevenson, Robert Louis, 39
strangles (gourme), 15, 16, 67, 88
Survival International, 120
Sylvéréal, 22

Tarn river, 44
Tassili n'Ajjer, 62
Taulé, 119
Telegraph Sunday Magazine, 4, 14, 17
Terrasson-la-Villedieu, 70
Tibesti mountains, 62
Tibet, 20
Tocantins river, 65

Torpoint ferry, 124
Toulouse, 57
Tour Carbonnière, 24
Tour du Valat, 17, 20
Trévézal Rock, 119, 123
Tschiffely, Aimé Felix, 33, 34
Tuareg, 62
Turquay, Jean-François and Rosalie, 5–9

Uccello, Paolo, 94
Usson-du-Poitou, 80

Van der Post, Laurens, 83
Veneti tribe, 111
Vergie, Comte Enguerand de, 85
Vergnes, Jean-Paul, 69, 70
vets, 15, 16, 67
Vezère river, 70
Vienne river, 79–97 (passim)
Villeneuve d'Aveyron, 53, 55, 66
Vin de Sable, 13
vultures, 64–6

Wadebridge, 119
Washington, 33
Welsh ponies, 111
Wilson, Vivien, 15
wolves, 58
Woman's Hour, 44, 57
Wood family, 8, 14, 17

Yanomami Indians, 19